HISTORIC FREDERICK COUNTY

The Story of Frederick & Frederick County

by Christopher N. Butler

A publication of the
Historical Society of Frederick County

HPNbooks
A division of Lammert Incorporated
San Antonio, Texas

DEDICATION

To my parents, Connie and Dave Butler, who raised me to love history and to be intellectually curious.

CONTENTS

First Edition

ISBN: 978-1-939300-82-9
Library of Congress Card Catalog Number: 2015935270

Historic Frederick County: The Story of Frederick & Frederick County

author: Dr. Christopher N. Butler
cover artist: Rebecca Pearl
contributing writer for sharing the heritage: Joe Goodpasture

HPNbooks

president: Ron Lammert
project manager: Igor Patrushev
administration: Donna M. Mata, Melissa G. Quinn
book sales: Dee Steidle
production: Colin Hart, Evelyn Hart, Glenda Tarazon Krouse, Tony Quinn

PRINTED IN THE UNITED STATES

FOREWORD

Preserving the history of Frederick County is a daunting task. The earliest documented era of occupation dates back at least 10,000 years ago, and Europeans began exploring the territory in the seventeenth century. The county's location made it a transportation crossroads, and over the centuries, a variety of new inhabitants made their mark on the county.

Major events in our nation's history had their impact here. The repudiation of the Stamp Act in 1765 preceded the more widely known Boston Tea Party and presaged the Revolutionary War. A century later, the county played a key role in the Civil War. In the twentieth century, the county became home to two internationally significant government sites. Camp David, located near Thurmont, has been a presidential retreat since Franklin D. Roosevelt was president. Fort Detrick, located in the county seat of Frederick, is a primary center for American biosecurity.

Accomplishing this formidable undertaking, Christopher Butler has distilled thousands of years of history into a concise summary, presented in chronological order. Tracing the county's settlement from pre-history through the twentieth century, he has captured the character of the county's residents, and the consequences of their actions, weaving together the experiences of many generations.

Included in this consummate account of life in Frederick County are profiles of businesses and other entities. The history of these participants is fleeting, reminding us of the transitory nature of our recorded history.

Although its size has diminished since it was formed in 1748, Frederick County remains today as the largest county in the state. The county's scenic views, stores and restaurants, communities, and the warmth of welcoming residents attract visitors from all over the world and compel them to stay.

Established in 1892, the Historical Society of Frederick County is a nonprofit educational organization with a mission to increase public awareness of, and appreciation for, the history of Frederick County. We welcome the participation of people of all ages and backgrounds. My thanks to Assistant Director Amanda Burdette Johnston and Research Center Coordinator Marian Currens for their help on this project. The board and staff of the Historical Society of Frederick County hope you find this publication to be a lasting and useful reference.

Executive Director Mary Rose Boswell
Historical Society of Frederick County

ACKNOWLEDGEMENTS

This book would not have been possible without the assistance and support of my wife, Kristen Butler, as well as Jennifer Winter and Carrie Blough, all of whom contributed much of the research for this book, and Duane Doxzen, who encouraged me to write it. Melissa Caples selected many of the pictures that are in the book. Expert fact-checkers, Nancy Lesure, Nancy Geasey, and Matthew Borders, helpfully scrutinized the work. Special thanks go to the staff of the Historical Society of Frederick County, past and present, particularly Research Center Coordinator Marian Currens. I also want to thank the innumerable volunteers at the Historical Society of Frederick County who provide the backbone of the organization and who have always been eager to help or talk during my time there. Thanks are also due to Ron Lammert, my contact at HPNbooks, who gave me the chance to contribute to the narrative of Frederick County's history. My grandparents, Denzil and Genevieve Butler and Arlie and Jean Kittle, taught me to value history and education. Finally, my cats Boxer and Sabrina kept me company during the writing and editing process.

Christopher N. Butler

✧ *The "clustered spires of Frederick": Trinity Chapel, Evangelical Lutheran Church, and St. John's Catholic Church.*

✧ *The Historical Society of Frederick County, c. 1960.*

✧ *Before it housed the Historical Society, the building housed the Loats Orphanage. This photograph shows the girls and Mrs. Hillary, who was matron from 1893–1927.*

PREFACE

Paths cross and roads meet in Frederick County. This Maryland county sits on many routes and borders, geographic and cultural, a trait that characterizes its history. It marks the boundary between eastern and western Maryland and sits on the division between the northern and southern United States. For thousands of years before European Contact, American Indians used the region's valleys and waterways as the foundation of vast trade networks, and after colonization roads, railroads, and canals connected Frederick County to the burgeoning United States. These boundaries and networks opened new possibilities for Frederick County's residents, as well as led vast conflicts to their doors. Their lives are preserved through stories, objects, and documents, which let us combine the ephemeral echoes of people into histories, whether of nations, states, families, or individuals.

Since its organization in 1892, the Historical Society of Frederick County has been the primary steward of these histories in the county. Since its origins as a private organization dedicated to nurturing a public passion for Frederick County's history, the Historical Society has brought enthusiasm and aptitude to the study of the region's past. Based on East Church Street in a building that has been a home and an orphanage, the Historical Society continues to preserve and to interpret Frederick County's history. Where the region's roads, railroads, and waterways continue to bridge geographical boundaries, the Historical Society bridges the past and the present with the possibilities of the future.

The Story of Frederick & Frederick County

NATIVE PEOPLE OF FREDERICK COUNTY

While Frederick is now best known for the city's "clustered spires," it is also a region rich in natural resources and beauty. Prior to European Contact, Native people found this bounty and made their lives here. Much about their lives and cultures is unknown, due to the devastating effects of colonialism and the limitations of archaeological research, but the pre-Columbian inhabitants of what is now Frederick County traded widely throughout eastern North America and utilized a variety of subsistence strategies to thrive in this region. The county's indigenous people inhabited a rich cultural and spiritual realm that explained the world as it existed, its origin, and their own place in it. They also lived in a rich social world composed of societies who thought about their lives and utilized their natural resources in a range of ways, changing often throughout time.

Frederick County's first inhabitants drew upon its rich natural resources in a variety of ways to meet their needs. As material culture and subsistence strategies are closely linked, archaeologists can provide detailed answers to how ancient people survived and often thrived in difficult environments. Among the earliest recognizable tool traditions in the Americas is that of the Paleo-Indians: a term referring to a range of societies spread across the continent roughly thirteen thousand years ago. Using fluted Clovis spear points, Paleo-Indians hunted North American megafauna, such as mammoths, while gathering a range of edible plants. They followed the migrations of game animals in highly mobile groups. Frederick County had a very different ecology during this period than it does today. Its forests were primarily composed of spruce and pine trees, much like Alaska in the early twenty-first century, and the waterways such as the Potomac River followed different courses in many places. While rare, there are examples of Paleo-Indian tools that have surfaced in Frederick County, although it is unclear when people first inhabited the region. If they were present during this period, cooling temperatures caused by climate change may have forced these groups out of his region for a time. Regardless of an earlier occupation, archaeological finds suggest that they lived here roughly eleven thousand years ago.

Warming temperatures led to new ways of life for Native people during the Early, Middle, and Late Archaic periods. Camps became larger and more developed, and new technologies, such as grindstones and pitted stones, opened up new resources for processing seeds and nuts. During the Archaic periods, North America's inhabitants weathered numerous shifts in climate and developed many distinctive tool traditions. By 2500 BCE, people in the Middle Atlantic region increasingly inhabited the area's broad flood plains. The Potomac River was a particularly rich source of quartzite, which was manufactured into large, stemmed points. The Early Woodland period, characterized by ceramic pottery used for cooking and storage, began around 1450 BCE. While this technology had been in use in southwestern North America for some time, it was a new innovation in this region, and many new forms and techniques developed over the next few centuries as potters experimented. Archaeologists also find more storage pits for food and supplies in this period, although whether this is because of an increasing need for them due to climate change or uncertain times, or if this simply reflects the use of larger, more archaeologically obvious pits is unclear.

Along with subsistence strategies, recovered artifacts suggest the existence of extensive trade networks from the Atlantic coast to the Ohio River Valley. These trade routes linked coastal peoples, who produced shell beads, to the mound-building cultures of the Adena along the Ohio River between 600 BCE and 100 CE. In exchange for shell beads, which were used as grave goods in the vast mortuary mounds built by the Adena, traders received goods such as tubular pipes and shale gorgets in return. Trade goods placed in burials on the Delmarva Peninsula provide evidence for this trading network. Valuable raw materials from what became Frederick County also entered into this network. One valuable resource found in Frederick County was rhyolite, a volcanic stone prized by toolmakers. Rhyolite was quarried at several sites along the Catoctin Ridge and tools were made from it there, the first instance of mass production in a region that would become characterized by industry

✧ *John White's 1590 portrayal of Pomeiock, a fortified Pamlico town in North Carolina. Although the organization of communities varied widely across pre-Contact North America, circular stockades were used in some indigenous communities in what became Frederick County.*

PUBLIC DOMAIN IMAGE. ORIGINAL OWNED BY THE BRITISH MUSEUM.

following its occupation by Euro-American settlers. These trade networks atrophied around 200 CE, but rhyolite remained valuable in the region. Large-scale trade reemerged around 700 CE, connecting western Maryland to such far-flung locations as New York, Ohio, and the Great Lakes region. This may have indicated a spread of Algonquian speakers from Lake Ontario, or the adoption of these languages, through these areas.

Around 1000 CE, maize, a major new resource, began to emerge in the Middle Atlantic region. Although cultivated for thousands of years in Mexico, selective breeding of maize in North America over a long period finally enabled the crop to thrive in the colder northern climate. This led to a greater emphasis on village life, and agricultural production became an important resource that eclipsed hunting and foraging. Many villages were located in floodplains for access to rich soil. An increasing numbers of stockaded villages after 1300 CE hint at a growing tension in the region, possibly due to a global climate shift that left eastern North America wetter and colder. With an increased reliance on maize as a dietary staple, this change damaged production and likely led to food scarcity.

✧ *John White's 1590 representation of a man from Pomeiock. He is wearing clothing appropriate for winter in the Carolinas and his community is visible in the background. Social organization and cultures varied widely throughout indigenous North America, but the Pamlico also spoke an Algonquian language and their clothing may have been similar to that worn by the indigenous inhabitants of the Chesapeake region.*

PUBLIC DOMAIN IMAGE. ORIGINAL OWNED BY THE BRITISH LIBRARY.

Although Europeans were present on the Middle Atlantic Coast by 1608 when John Smith described the village Natotchtanks at the mouth of the Anacostia River, few traveled inland and no records describe the Native people of western Maryland in the early seventeenth century. Smith, who turned back at the Falls of the Potomac—which he named for the Patawomekes, another Native group in the region—tells us that these groups were Algonquian speakers, with Siouan and Iroquoian languages also spoken. During this period, Frederick County formed part of the southern border of the Five Nations of the Iroquois Confederacy, a powerful multi-tribal coalition stretching from the eastern Great Lakes through New York. Of the members of the Confederacy, the Seneca and Shawnee were particularly influential in western Maryland, as a major north-south trade route passed through Frederick County. This borderland region was also home to other tribal nations, including those displaced by European colonization. In 1699, many Piscataway settled in the region after being falsely accused of violence against white and black Maryland colonists. They established a settlement on Heaters Island before moving into Pennsylvania by 1712 after a smallpox epidemic. Tuscarora refugees lived along the Potomac near the mouth of the Monocacy River in the eighteenth century following their 1713 military defeat by an alliance of South Carolinian and Cherokee forces. In 1719, they sold ten thousand acres of their land to an English settler, Charles Carroll, and continued north. Both of these groups eventually became part of the Iroquois Confederacy.

Such population shifts and movements were common as European settlements emerged on the Atlantic Coast and European diseases decimated Native populations. With no resistance to lethal diseases like smallpox, many American Indians died from illness. Estimates for these deaths are high, such as that given by historian Henry Dobyns, who suggested that the mortality rate could have been eighty or ninety percent. While these numbers are highly debated, and varied by region and time period, the secondary effects of European Contact, such as disease, famine, and warfare, changed Native communities forever. The loss of so many people to disease led to famines as survivors struggled to work fields with too few people and populations shifted as communities merged and moved in response to these events. These migrations spread new illnesses further, and American Indian populations were often decimated before meeting colonists face-to-face. This contributed to a sense of divine entitlement for colonists, who thanked God for their new, fertile land, little realizing that these were fields worked by generations of Native people. At the same time, many Native Americans questioned their own religious beliefs when faced with these tragedies, sometimes making conversion to Christianity easier for missionaries. The cultural fabric of these communities was devastated, as oral knowledge was lost.

At the same time, American Indians became enmeshed in global trade networks, with furs eagerly sought by British and French traders acquiring goods for a seemingly endless European market for beaver hides. Never passive victims of these events, American Indians actively entered this new political and economic environment and many tribal nations gained European allies. Both Europeans and American Indians used these allegiances in existing conflicts with other colonial or tribal powers. John Smith noted this, when he reported that the Algonquian speakers he interacted with were concerned with Susquehannock raids throughout New York and Pennsylvania. The Susquehannock were already embedded in global trade networks, as Smith discovered when he met them trading French goods in the northern Chesapeake Bay region.

European Contact was felt in individual lives, which caused ripples in the diplomatic relationships between European and tribal nations. One case occurred in the Monocacy (or Manakassy) Valley with the murder of Sawantaeny, a Seneca man, by John and Edmund Cartlidge, a pair of colonial traders. This death provides a unique window into the violence that European traders brought to this region. The killing was reconstructed during a hearing by Pennsylvania officials on March 14, 1722, held at Conestoga, a Susquehanna village under Iroquois control with a multi-tribal population. This hearing was recorded in the *Minutes of the Provincial Council of Pennsylvania*. Witnesses described Sawantaeny as a civil, quiet warrior, who was hunting near the "Manakassy, a Branch of [the] Patomeck River," accompanied by Weynepreeueyta, his Shawnee wife, who was a witness at the hearing. Her testimony, and that of the Cartlidge's Indian guide, suggests that John and Edmund Cartlidge, with their Indian guides and white servants, arrived at Sawantaeny and Weynepreeueyta's cabin one evening to trade for furs. As a gift, likely to show respect for their host, the Cartlidges gave Sawantaeny some punch and rum throughout the evening.

The next morning a dispute about payment, which included rum, became heated. John knocked Sawantaeny onto a fallen log. With blood running down his neck, Sawantaeny retrieved his gun from the cabin while Weynepreeueyta tried to diffuse the situation. Edmund wrestled the gun away from Sawantaeny and repeatedly struck him in the head with it, eventually breaking the firearm. John kicked Sawantaeny in the side and broke two ribs. Sawantaeny was left bleeding from the nose and mouth and unable to speak as the traders packed their goods and left. Before he died the following morning Sawantaeny's last words were that "his friends had killed him." His surprise is evident in this statement, suggesting that this was the tragic culmination of a long-term trading relationship. After Sawantaeny's death, Weynepreeueyta left to find help for the burial. In her absence a Cayuga man found his body and hired the leader of Conestoga's wife and "the Hermaphrodite of that same place" to bury him, likely as mourners in a ritual capacity as historian Gunlög Fur suggests. Although eastern North American examples are rare, this hermaphrodite was likely a man who dressed and lived as a woman. Many Midwestern tribal nations recognized a similar social role, often known as a berdache.

✧ *Another 1590 drawing by John White, this time of a community on the Pamlico River estuary, also in North Carolina. While also not in Frederick County, this town shows the potential variations in special organization within a region.*

PUBLIC DOMAIN IMAGE. ORIGINAL OWNED BY THE BRITISH MUSEUM.

This deeply personal affair quickly achieved an international element. News of Sawantaeny's death was heard by the Maryland council at Annapolis on February 21, 1722. The council's records note that John Bradford, a man familiar with the event, suggested that Sawantaeny was prominent within the Seneca and had been killed "by making a violent stroke at his head with the Indian's own Gun and drove the head of the Cock into his Brains." The Pennsylvania council's minutes noted the issue on March 6, 1722, a month after the death. With the Maryland council encouraging colonists to "let the Indians know that the Murderers are under the PA Government," Pennsylvania's council, eager to find "the most effectual and cheapest way to preserve [the Indians'] friendship, and to quell any Disturbance which hereafter may possibly happen upon such extraordinary Events," sent forth a delegation. The council secretary John Logan and a military officer, Colonel French, located John Cartlidge in Conestoga and began the hearing, along with a variety of prominent Conestoga men, including Shawnee, Mingo, Ganawese, Conestoga, and Delaware representatives. During the hearing, which was conducted in at least five languages with Delaware being common language of translation, the sad tale of the murder was told over eight hours.

The Pennsylvania council attempted to make reparations to the Seneca for Sawataeny's death, likely fearing the consequences of alienating the powerful League of the Iroquois. Logan and French distributed rum punch, as well as John Carlidge's meat and bread, throughout Conestoga. They offered a symbolic gift to the Seneca of two blankets "to cover our dead friend [Sawantaeny]" and a valuable wampum belt "to wipe away Tears." Following multiple trials, the Cartlidges were ultimately released after the head of the Confederacy stated that he felt sorry for Sawantaeny's death, but "he desires that John Cartlidge may not be put to death; one life is enough to be lost, there should not two die." However, the Cartlidges were forbidden from future trade with American Indians, and Pennsylvania's traders were prevented from trading rum with them, to prevent further destabilization of the delicate diplomatic relationships with the tribal nations. This incident shows the uneasy and at times violent nature of even friendship in the colonial borderlands, and the need to maintain peaceful relationships with the members of the Five Nations of the Iroquois, who wielded extensive authority.

Although most regional tribes were relocated, often as their land was seized or fraudulently purchased by European colonists, these tribal histories continue. Many Piscataway eventually settled in Canada on the Six Nations of the Grand River First Nation reserve in Ontario after moving on from Heaters Island. Other Piscataway remained largely unrecognized in Maryland until the late nineteenth century when many identified themselves to scholars and journalists. After legal struggles for government recognition, three Piscataway descendant groups were recognized by the state of Maryland in December 2011: the Piscataway Indian Nation and Tayac Territory, the Piscataway Conoy Tribe of Maryland, and the Cederville Band of Piscataway Indians.

As with the Piscataway, the Tuscarora split into different migrations as a result of the colonial period. After the Tuscarora moved north out of Frederick County due to tensions with European settlers, many settled in New York. Their recognized descendants still live there as members of the federally recognized Tuscarora Nation, while others live on the Six Nations reserve in Ontario. Some Tuscarora returned to North Carolina, while others joined with displaced Seneca and Cayuga people as the Mingo, and have descendants within the Seneca-Cayuga Tribe of Oklahoma. Most Seneca, as British allies, moved to Canada following the American Revolution, where their descendants also live on the Six Nations reserve, with other recognized descendants located in New York and Oklahoma.

Many Shawnee lived in Frederick County, including those who helped the French fur trader Martin Chartier set up trade routes through the region. Following Shawnee leader Tecumseh's multi-tribal military campaign, the bulk of the Shawnee Nation was located in Ohio, where they ceded their remaining lands to the United States for three reservations in the state. By 1833 most were removed by the U.S. government to Kansas, and after the Civil War, were moved again to the Indian Territory, now the state of Oklahoma. Here they joined other Shawnee, who had moved to Texas in the early nineteenth century. Some Kansas Shawnee were settled within the Cherokee Nation and were part of that tribe until 2000, when they received separate federal recognition. Other Shawnee descendants, some with state recognition, reside in Ohio. Although the Native population of Frederick County is low in the twenty-first century, vibrant American Indian communities persist throughout Maryland. In Baltimore, for instance, a large multi-tribal urban Indian population developed during the mid-twentieth century, as many sought economic opportunities in the burgeoning shipbuilding industry.

✧ *While many of the material remains of this period are gone, many memorial observations of the colonial period have occurred in Frederick County. In this image from 1922, county residents observe the 190th anniversary of the building of the Old Monocacy Log Church and the later organization of the Old Monocacy Reformed Church.*

EUROPEAN COLONIZATION

By the early 1720s, European colonists were beginning to enter the region. Most of these colonists were attracted to the rich farmland, which caused tension and conflict with American Indians. Roughly sixty percent of these early settlers were British and the remaining forty percent were largely German, along with some Swiss and Scotch-Irish. The German settlers served as a buffer between British and French territorial claims. These settlers farmed grains, which were milled into flour, and manufactured goods including lime, iron, and glass. The need for a central economic and political site emerged, and Daniel Dulaney, a land speculator and a member of Maryland's colonial government, purchased Tasker's Chance, a large tract of land in the Monocacy Valley where he established Frederick in 1745. Dulaney sold individual lots to settlers. The first purchasers were John Thomas Schley and his wife Margaret from the German Rhine. John Thomas, who had been a schoolmaster in Germany, established a tavern in Frederick. He was also active as a musician in the German Reformed Church. With the church, he served as a schoolmaster and a lay leader. The Schleys retained connections to Germany, often writing to encourage friends to join them in Frederick.

By 1748 the increased settler population led the colonial government to establish Frederick County as a separate area. The county was much larger then and covered most of western Maryland, including current-day Garrett, Allegheny, Washington, Frederick, and Montgomery Counties, as well as part of Carroll County. With this growth, Frederick became a center for grain shipments to Baltimore, which led to the development of major transportation routes through the county. Many of these roads traveled east-west, linked to Baltimore and the coast. This east-west orientation persisted after the American Revolution, with the National Road, the Baltimore and Ohio Railroad, and the Chesapeake and Ohio Canal all passing through the county.

In the mid-eighteenth century, Frederick and Washington Counties were on the western edge of the English colonies, sharing a border with numerous tribal nations and with French territories to the west. As British colonists pushed westward toward the Ohio River Valley, this threatened French claims. In the spring of 1754, a freshly minted lieutenant colonial in the Virginia militia, George Washington, was

✧ *According to local tradition, this cabin on Saint Street in Frederick, which was in disrepair when photographed in the nineteenth century, was briefly used by George Washington as a headquarters during the French and Indian War.*

✧ *The spring that Braddock allegedly stopped at on his way west became a local landmark in Frederick County. Here a man and a young boy pose at the site.*

sent west to defend an English fort on the Ohio River. While travelling through western Pennsylvania, Washington and his men engaged a party of French soldiers, which escalated into the French and Indian War in 1755. This war represented the North American expansion of the Seven Years' War—a series of ongoing hostilities between England and France. On this new front, not only were colonial forces brought into the war, but tribal nations used the broader war to reshape their relationships with European powers or to continue existing hostilities within Native North America. Many tribal nations, including the Shawnee, sided with the French to resist English settlements, although others remained British allies.

In response the British military commander in colonial North America, General Edward Braddock, brought 1,400 British soldiers to the colonies for a military expedition in March 1755. They passed through Frederick on to the French Fort Duquesne, near what is now Pittsburgh, Pennsylvania. According to legend as Braddock left Frederick, he stopped to drink at a spring on the ridge west of town, which is now called Braddock Heights. The colonial governments of Virginia and Maryland provided only about ten percent of the horses and wagons Braddock requested. Benjamin Franklin was sent to calm Braddock, and he contracted for these supplies in Pennsylvania. This logistical problem delayed Braddock's departure until April, as many western settlers, worried about the increasing violence in the region, took refuge in Frederick. In May, on his way to meet Braddock in Winchester, Virginia, George Washington stayed overnight in Frederick. Braddock led his forces west into the mountains to a military staging area at Fort Cumberland, near Will's Creek—a British community that had been a Shawnee village. This is now Cumberland, Maryland. Tensions between the British, the French, and the tribal nations continued to escalate. In the June 12, 1755, issue of the *Maryland Gazette*, Governor Shirley advertised cash bounties for American Indian prisoners and scalps, including those of women and children. Later that month, a French offensive began near Fort Cumberland and, by early July, twenty-eight British colonists had been killed or captured in western Maryland.

Braddock's forces collided with the French and their allies on July 9 near Fort Duquesne, a battle that was disastrous for the British. Roughly 900 of Braddock's 1,400 men were killed, wounded, or captured during the battle. This included Braddock himself, who was mortally wounded in the fighting and who died on July 13. That day, his fleeing forces had camped near Fort Necessity, Washington's makeshift defenses from his initial clash with the French. After Braddock's death, and possibly at Washington's suggestion, his soldiers supposedly buried Braddock in the road and marched over the grave to conceal it from the French and their allies.

Charlotte Brown, a woman attached to the Braddock expedition, wrote about these events in her diary. She arrived at Fort Cumberland on June 13, 1755, describing it as "the most desolate Place I ever saw." Conditions at the fort were sparse, Brown called her lodging a "hole," in which she "could see day light through every Log and a port Hole for a Window which was as good a Room as any in the Fort." While she was there, news of Indian violence reached the fort, leading the gates to be shut against a group of "several [individuals] who called themselves friendly Indians." This incident highlights the ambiguity of British relations with Native people. Word came on July 11, 1755, of Braddock's defeat. Brown stated that "it is not possible to describe the Distraction of the poor Women for their Husbands." Shortly thereafter, Brown's brother died of illness and she left for Frederick, a 150-mile journey. Brown found the prospect daunting, noting that "God only knows how I shall get there." During the trip, she faced many difficulties, including a fall from her horse into the Potomac River and sleeping on the ground—which she referred to as "my old lodging"—but arrived in Frederick on August 30.

Frederick was a welcome sight for Brown. Following her recovery from a fever, Brown explored Frederick. She described the town as "a very Pleasant Place [where] most of the People are Dutch." Brown received a series of invitations while she waited for the remainder of the sick to arrive from the fort. She visited numerous country estates in the area, including one in which she "was received with a friendly welcome [and] I had for Breakfast a fine Dish of Fish and a Pig." Her sensibilities were shocked at a ball, an incident that shows Frederick's diverse population and the blending of cultures that characterized colonial frontier life. She described the ball as "compos'd of Romans, Jews, and Hereticks [sic] who in this Town flock together. The Ladys [sic] danced without Stays or Hoops and it ended with a jig from each [Lady?]." On October 5, all of the fort's sick had arrived, along with news of further violence and a lack of supplies at the fort. In a scene repeated during the American Civil War, Frederick became a military hospital, where the wounded and ill from Braddock's campaign were tended before continuing to Philadelphia on October 11. Brown left Frederick with them.

Other sources suggest the undercurrents of fear in Frederick County during the French and Indian War. Given these concerns, in 1756, Fort Frederick was constructed on the orders of Governor Sharp to protect the region's settlers. It was one of the first stone forts built in the southern provinces. This violence was not one-sided. Reprisals by Indian combatants not only took place within the broader international war, but also within a context in which Indian men, women, and children were being targeted for capture or death by colonial authorities.

THE AMERICAN REVOLUTION

Following the French and Indian War, tensions rose between the colonies and the British government due to higher taxes imposed to offset the additional debts incurred in defending the colonies. These policies led the colonial leadership to split from Britain, precipitating the American Revolution. Many of these British policies were unpopular in Frederick County. Following the passage of the Stamp Act of 1765, an act that contained a provision that court business must be conducted on properly stamped paper, Frederick County judges used unstamped paper rather than close courts. This was followed by a mock funeral procession and burial for the distributor of Maryland stamps, Zachariah Hood, which included a coffin and an effigy. This demonstration was held by a local branch of the Sons of Liberty. Western Maryland delegates to the Continental Congress also unanimously supported the split from Britain.

Many Frederick County men joined militias to support the revolutionary cause, likely swept up in a patriotic fervor. On December 8, 1774, an act was passed in Frederick enabling the organization of military companies for the brewing conflict. With this act, men between the ages of sixteen and fifty began to enlist. With the outbreak of the war at Lexington and Concord on April 19, 1775, two Frederick County companies rushed to join the fighting in Boston. These companies joined Captain Daniel Morgan's men from Shepherdstown, Virginia (now West Virginia), as they traveled through Frederick on July 17. When this combined group reached Boston, they were the first southern troops to join the battle. Shortly thereafter, the Maryland Line was organized, which was composed of four companies from Frederick County—of which three were from Emmitsburg—and two to three companies from Montgomery County. The Maryland Line fought at Brooklyn Heights in New York City on July 4, 1776. Following the colonists' retreat from New York, the Maryland Line guarded British and Hessian prisoners of war held in Frederick. By 1781 the Line had taken such heavy losses that it had to be reorganized, which resulted in the loss of three regiments. Another prominent Frederick County company was organized as part of the German Regiment by the Maryland General Assembly in July 1776. This regiment was formed of two companies, the other being from Baltimore. The regiment's members served until 1780 and fought at Trenton, White Plains, and Brandywine before being folded into the Maryland Continental Troops in January 1781. County residents also supported the revolutionary cause financially, although a letter from Continental Congress delegate John Hanson suggested that the support may have been primarily among the county's elite more than lower-class civilians, as he found resistance in getting people to part with their gold and silver unless it was replaced by paper tender.

✧ *Rose Hill Manor, where Thomas Carroll spent his twilight years.*

✧ Thomas Johnson and Family, *by Charles Willson Peale.*

Frederick County also provided revolutionary leaders, including numerous members of the Continental Congress. As a Continental Congress delegate, Thomas Johnson was on the Committee of Correspondence to seek foreign aid for the revolutionary cause. He also served in the Maryland assembly and was a brigadier general in the state militia. He became the state's first governor in 1777, served on the commission that laid out Washington, D.C., and sat on the Supreme Court. Following his years in public service, he lived out his life in Frederick at Rose Hill Manor, his daughter and son-in-law's estate. Another prominent Frederick County resident during the revolution was Charles Carroll, who was a Continental Congress representative, as well as the only Catholic to sign the Declaration of Independence. He went on to a career in government, serving in both the Maryland and U.S. senates. Other Frederick residents also served in the Continental Congress, including John Hanson, who was the first president of Congress to serve a full one-year term following the ratification of the Articles of Confederation, and Thomas Sim Lee, who was Maryland's governor during the ratification of the Articles of Confederation.

Other county residents actively resisted the revolution. A group of seven Frederick County men were arrested and three were executed in 1781 for attempting to raise volunteers and to acquire weapons for the British. This loyalist plot, seemingly led by John Caspar Fritchie (or Frietschie)—the father-in-law of famed Civil War figure Barbara Fritchie, was revealed by Christian Orendorff, who ostensibly joined the plot to turn them over to the Americans, and much of our knowledge of the plot comes from his testimony. Henry Newcomer, another conspirator, met with Orendorff and asked him about his position on the war and if the British would win it. Orendorff described Newcomer's stated goal this way: "We have raised a Body of Men for the Service of the King and we thought proper to make [application] to you to go to [New] York for a Fleet, asked how many Men they had raised he said upwards of 6,000—asked who was the Commanding officer of the Party, answered one Fritchy of Fred. Town a Dutch man." Orendorff was then introduced to Fritchie, who provided more details, and Bleacher, a captain in the conspiracy, who claimed he had recruited fifty men. According to Orendorff, Bleacher then revealed further details of the plot:

> Bleacher said they would mount on Horses and ride down [to Georgetown] and receive their arms for the troops in the State would not hinder them—and further said he could take the Magazine in Fred. Town with their Men.

Following this revelation, seven men were arrested and Fritchie and two others were sentenced to be drawn and quartered, a punishment often handed down for traitors. As in other cases in colonial Maryland, it appears as if these sentences were commuted to hanging, which was what happened to these three men on July 6, 1781. Local tradition holds that Fritchie was innocent and was linked to the conspirators through business ties, and that his wife received a pardon for him from George Washington—which would not have been applicable as this was a civil rather than military matter—that arrived too late to stop his execution. However, there is no evidence that this version is true. The earliest written form of this version dates from the Civil War, likely as a result of Barbara Fritchie's sudden fame. Orendorff's account may not be completely accurate, either, and he may have exaggerated the danger posed by Fritchie's conspiracy to make his role in the revolution seem more prominent.

As in later wars, Frederick County not only supplied soldiers and funds, but also harnessed its manufacturing capabilities for the struggle. In the summer of 1775, the Maryland government contracted five Frederick County gunsmiths to manufacture firearms for the war effort. One of these gunsmiths was George Boon, who produced firearms in Frederick's Cannon Hill industrial district. Later that year, the Maryland government also established a Frederick County manufactory to produce gunlocks, which was closed in 1778. Not only were Frederick County guns beginning to be used across the colony, but by 1776 local militia captains relied on them to supply their forces. Both George Stricker and Thomas Johnson requested funds from Annapolis that year to purchase muskets, with Johnson writing "considering the difficulty of speedily arming our troops I think with them & will [be] advisable to lodge a sum of money in the hands of somebody here...to purchase what rifles can be got." Early in the war, many Maryland troops relied on their Frederick County-produced rifles, although production declined as the war progressed. While the iron works at Catoctin Furnace did not produce guns, the iron workers did manufacture war materiel, such as cast shell and shot, as well as military camping supplies.

As firearm production lessened, the county's role as a major agricultural center came to the forefront. In December 1779 the Maryland General Assembly directed commissioners to buy all the grains that exceeded the needs of merchants and farmers in order to provide flour and food to the Continental Army. The Maryland council wrote to Frederick County's procurement officer, Colonel Normand Bruce, instructing him to use every method to get the needed flour. This even extended to exchanging gunpowder for small quantities of wheat at mills, with one bushel of wheat worth one pound of gunpowder. Another commissioner, Thomas Price, gathered one-and-a-half bushels of wheat at twenty-two pounds, ten shillings per bushel from one Frederick farmer. As a result, in 1780, many farmers harvested their grain early for export, although this was difficult due to insufficient transportation caused by the war.

Frederick County also held many prisoners of war from the British army. Early in the war, the legislature proposed the construction of a jail in Frederick to house military captives, which was accepted by a local committee who desired a central location so the structure could be used as a school after the war. This facility was known as the Tory or log jail. Throughout the war, the jail posed difficulties for the town, particularly due to insufficient guards and supplies. In December 1777 newly arrived British prisoners were housed in a smaller public jail rather than the new prison due to a lack of guards. Even after the public jail was set on fire during an escape attempt, Charles Beatty, the prison's head, could not find enough guards. After moving the prisoners to the prison, Beatty and a skeleton crew of guards watched them for a week before Thomas Johnson requisitioned sufficient men for the task.

These problems were just the beginning. In December 1780, British prisoners from the battle of Saratoga began to arrive, who would eventually number over seven hundred, a sizeable number for a town with a population of roughly 1,700. The prisoners were held there until the next summer and supply problems persisted. One resident, Baker Johnson, wrote that "the whole neighborhood is continually plundered," seemingly by prisoners and guards. Later, in 1781, the prisoner population of Frederick boomed

✧ *Colonel Friedrich Heinrich Scheer commanded two regiments of Hessians during the revolution and was imprisoned in Frederick during the war.*

✧ *The Hessian Barracks in the last half of the nineteenth century.*

after the British surrender at Yorktown, Virginia. Shortages of willing guards and provisions arose again until the prisoners were sent to Pennsylvania in December. Early in 1782, new prisoners arrived in Frederick, who were to become strongly linked to the prison barracks in the public's memory. These prisoners, Hessian soldiers captured at Yorktown, arrived in January 1782. The Hessians were mercenaries from the Hesse region of Germany hired by the British. Many of these prisoners felt a strong affinity to Frederick County's German inhabitants. One Hessian prisoner, Johann Conrad Dohla, described Frederick in his journal in January 1782:

> [A] beautiful, fertile, and pleasant region, partially in a valley; however, when it rains, it becomes muddy because the city is still not paved. It is heavily settled by Germans, of whom many are from Swabia. This city was laid out sixteen years ago, but already has nearly two thousand inhabitants, has several good houses, and makes a show with several steeples. The streets of the city are laid out evenly, to the four corners of the world. A few houses are of wood, most of limestone and brick, both building materials that are baked and prepared here. The inhabitants carry on handcrafts and agriculture.

With few capable guards, whose ranks now included injured veterans, prisoners frequently escaped. Some Hessian escapees married local women and started families, leading many to stay after the war. Given widespread escapes, the Continental Congress eventually allowed the married prisoners in question to be freed for a fee. Other problems were more difficult and could lead to violence. One prisoner was shot during an escape attempt, which was an exception to the generally lax imprisonment. Others, including two paroled British officers and three of their Hessian visitors, were beaten by a gang led by Dr. Adam Fischer, a revolutionary leader. While violence and conflict was not uncommon in the prison, these later events were seemingly outliers, with most crime in the barracks the result of prisoners and guards coping with their limited supplies in illicit ways.

Not everyone in Frederick Town viewed the prisoners as threatening or problematic; others saw an opportunity. Given that as many as one quarter of the male population of the county was away in the war, labor was at a premium. As early as February 1778, Beatty suggested that the use of British POWs for labor benefited both the prisoners and the county's residents, stating that the prisoners "could get themselves some little necessaries & be of great use in the neighborhood of this place." This outsourcing would allow him to manage troublesome prisoners more easily, given his continuing lack of guards. In early 1781, British prisoners chopped firewood, given the extreme pressures the prisoners placed on local supplies. Later that year the Maryland council suggested that the British prisoners from Yorktown could be put to this use. However, the arrival of the Hessian soldiers to the prison revealed a new dimension of prisoner labor in Frederick County. Bayly, the officer in charge of the prison, restricted access to the POWs to stop county residents from taking prisoners from the facility, seemingly as

✧ *Jacob Engelbrecht (1797–1878), pictured here c. 1865–1868, was a tailor and a diarist whose writings provide the broadest account of Frederick's nineteenth century history from 1818–1878. Engelbrecht also served as Frederick's mayor in the aftermath of the Civil War from 1865–1868.*

laborers. This angered residents and many petitioned the governor to intervene. He did not, and in 1782 a further edict made it illegal to house prisoners, which was punishable by a large fine—service on a ship for three years, or thirty-nine lashes. When the Continental Congress ruling was issued to free Hessians married to American women with a fine, military recruiters visited the barracks containing the Hessians with money and women, while local merchants used this ruling to purchase Hessian freedom in exchange for labor.

As the presence and activities of Revolutionary War POWs indicates, these men had a surprising amount of freedom, whether intentionally or inadvertently, and became a part of the community. Imprisoned officers had more latitude than enlisted soldiers. At the end of the war, many of these prisoners took part in the festivities marking American independence. Hessian diarist Johann Conrad Dohla recorded that American soldiers and militiamen built a large bonfire and marched through Frederick Town "behind the resounding sounds of fifes and drums through all of the streets and ways of this place with white flags, green caps, and laurel wreaths on their heads, and firing their weapons," all while cheering "Hyroh for Peace! Hyroh for liberty!" The local artillery, headed by Captain Nikolaus Friedrich Hoffman, fired a cannon from a nearby elevation and presented an elaborate fireworks display. Dohal records:

> When this was all finished, a splendid ball was held in a large hall, attended by all the American officers and all of the gentlemen and rich merchants of the city. They ate, drank, and danced the entire night to the music of our and the Hesian hautboists. All the officers of the captive regiments were invited to this dance of joy and celebration of peace. All the Hessians attended, but from our two regiments, only Lt. von Ciriacy participated.

Many Hessian soldiers remained in Frederick County after the war, having found a pleasant life among the region's German settlers. Of the thirty thousand Hessian soldiers who fought in the American Revolution, only seventeen thousand returned to Germany. One of those who stayed was Conrad Engelbrecht, the father of Jacob Engelbrecht, an important nineteenth-century Frederick County diarist.

POST-REVOLUTIONARY FREDERICK COUNTY

After American independence, farming continued to dominate Frederick County's economy. Outside Frederick, most county residents were farmers. With a favorable climate and soil, wheat became the county's major agricultural product after Charles Carroll of Carrollton encouraged regional farmers to adopt it late in the colonial period. Other grains, including barley, oats, and rye, were also raised, as were limited quantities of tobacco. Due to the climate and the soil, which was quite different from the Eastern Shore, tobacco remained a volatile product in Frederick County and never became a significant export. With all of this agricultural activity, the Frederick County Agricultural Society was organized in 1821.

✧ *Agricultural production of grains such as wheat and barley remained central to the county's economy throughout the nineteenth century and into the twentieth. In this image, farmers use a horse-drawn grain binder during the harvest.*

During this period, Frederick County's agricultural basis contributed to the region's industrial development. Andrew and David Shriver built the Union Mills complex, which included a store, a saw mill, a brick kiln, a blacksmith, and a tannery. Many mills and distilleries converted regional farmers' produce into finished products. These operations processed grains into flour and meal, as well as distilled alcohol, all of which were easier to transport. These mills were powered by the many sources of water in the county, and they were constructed using the region's natural resources, particularly abundant timber and stones. In 1810, Frederick and Washington Counties produced roughly $1.5 million of milled goods, more than all Maryland's other counties combined. This regional orientation toward milling continued throughout the early nineteenth century. According to the census of 1820, one quarter of all Marylanders employed in manufacturing lived in these two counties. For more than a century mills were the principal regional manufacturers. Many mills operated before the revolution, early examples including Henry Ballenger's operation at Ballenger Creek by 1729 and the Davis Mill, later known as Michael's Mill, near Buckeystown in 1739. By 1798, Frederick County had over eighty flour and grist mills, as well as between three hundred and four hundred stills. The number of flour mills in the county had increased to 101 by 1810, which was more than in any other Maryland county. Frederick County

✧ *Jeffrey Hurwitz's mill on Easterday Road, c. mid- to late-nineteenth century.*

distilleries processed large amounts of alcohol. In 1810 distillers produced over 350 thousand gallons of alcohol from fruits and grains. Welty's South Mountain Distillery likely originated in the 1790s.

The agricultural lifestyle that provided the raw materials for the mills was a difficult and time-consuming enterprise. Even on the largest farms, all family members contributed to it. Farmers often relied on temporary laborers, both free and slave. While free laborers were hired, slaves were rented to other farmers by their owners. Slave ownership was dictated more by wealth than ethnicity, as affluent German and British residents owned slaves. While race-based slavery was not as prevalent in Frederick County as in other Southern regions, the percentage of county residents owned as slaves increased from twelve percent in 1790 to seventeen percent in 1820. Following this, the county's slave population declined, eventually reaching seven percent by 1860. Even though these proportions are relatively low, there were still thousands of people enslaved in the county. In 1830, diarist Jacob Engelbrecht noted that there were 533 slaves in Frederick, which was not the largest slaveholding area of the county. This grim distinction ironically belonged to Liberty. The census of 1860 lists more than three thousand slaves in the county, out of a total county population over forty-six thousand. The latter number also included almost five thousand free blacks. By the mid-1800s, the vast majority of slave owners were farmers. Higher-income occupations, like doctors and merchants, made up the next highest category. The remaining slave owners came from a range of occupations, from carpenters to lawyers.

By the beginning of the American republic, slavery already had a long history in Maryland. Indentured servants from Europe and Africa were among the first settlers in the Maryland colony in the 1630s. Indentured servants were not strictly slaves—but were individuals who exchanged a set period of labor for transportation to the colonies—and included a range of ethnicities, including both Europeans and Africans. This system bore similarities to slavery and became linked to race-based slavery in Maryland. In 1664 the Maryland colonial government decreed that people of African origin and their children were slaves for life, a decision that was made partly to fill the need for labor in the Eastern Shore's tobacco fields. While African slaves continued to be imported throughout the eighteenth century, the Act Prohibiting Importation of Slaves of 1807 made it illegal to bring new slaves into the United States. However, the United States' massive enslaved population allowed this cruel institution to continue to thrive, particularly in the South. In Frederick County, some early settlers from the

✧ *The second blacksmith shop in Woodsboro, c. late nineteenth century, owned by the Donsife brothers. Dan Zimerman stands next to the horse and cart, while Francis Genoa Donsife and Atho Donsife stand in front of the shop.*

✧ *Tanneries employed Frederick County residents from the eighteenth through the twentieth centuries. This image shows an employee of Birely Tannery at work.*

COURTESY OF FRAN RANDALL COLLECTION.

Eastern Shore desired to produce tobacco. These settlers brought their slaves with them. Although not the county's only slave owners, tobacco producers contributed to the early expansion of the slave population here. Licksville became an early center for the slave trade where George Kephart ran a well-known slave market. A contemporary described the way families were split by Kephart this way: "A father to a South Carolina planter, his wife to a Georgia Dealer and the children scattered among buyers." Breaking of enslaved families across state lines was common within the trade and was one of the many ways in which slavery destroyed families, communities, and lives.

Throughout the early years of the republic, there were many ways that people were enslaved in America. Most obviously, many were born into slavery. Due to the racial nature of slavery in the United States, slavery was passed to children by their mothers, without regard to the father's enslaved status. In this way, the children of a free man, whether black or white, and an enslaved woman became slaves themselves. Even free blacks could be forced into slavery by abduction or as punishment. Free blacks had to register with their local government and carry passes to prove their status. If free blacks did not possess their passes, slave catchers could abduct them. Sometimes people caught in this way were released by authorities if they could prove their status, such as through the testimony of friends or associates. Jacob Engelbrecht described such an event in his diary on June 12, 1825:

> This morning I appeared before George Rohr Esquire and made oath according to law "That I knew Negro Lott Jones for fifteen years and upwards and that he was always considered free born and that I knew his parents for the same period of time, and that they were always reputed as free and are now so." The above was done to procure Lott Jones, a certificate of his freedom from the clerk of Frederick County Court.

Free blacks who committed crimes were also at risk of being forced into slavery by the authorities. Black men jailed for vagrancy could be sold into slavery for a period of time. One Frederick County couple, a free black man and a white woman, faced this possibility when the man was sold into slavery in the Deep South.

Just as there were many ways to become a slave, there were many ways slaves became free. This was a rare occurrence. Most remained slaves all their lives, forced to labor for their masters, never able to experience the freedom that was ostensibly promised by the U.S. Constitution, and continually at the risk of violence at the hands of their masters. Some masters practiced manumission, which was a promise to free their slaves after a specified period of time. While this may appear selfless initially, there were practical reasons for masters to make and to keep these promises to their slaves. Some masters practiced it to gradually reduce the number of slaves they owned. Others used manumission to remove older slaves, individuals that the master would have to provide for if the slaves remained their property. Finally, others knew that their slaves were aware of the chance of freedom in free states. This was a major concern in the slave state of Maryland with the free state of Pennsylvania so very close. However, slaves with the promise of manumission might not risk the dangers of escape, but choose to wait to be freed after the appointed time. Others were willing to take this risk, and some slaves freed themselves by escaping and fleeing to a free state. With Pennsylvania close, many Maryland slaves attempted this. As running away was very perilous, most runaway slaves were young adult men. This was a very difficult decision, as runaways not only risked their lives, but also knew that running away would likely forever separate them from their families and other enslaved loved ones. Even with these barriers, many Frederick County slaves did escape. Many of these escapees went to Philadelphia, according to Abolitionist Society member William Still. One such successful escapee was John McPherson's slave, Ruthie Harper. While some slaves were helped by the abolitionist network known as the Underground Railroad, the majority of escapees made the attempt on their own. Finally, as a result of the Civil War, the slave population of the United States was freed through emancipation, or immediate freedom. During the war, slaves were emancipated in two waves. The 1863 Emancipation Proclamation freed all slaves in Confederate states, a policy that did not apply to slaves in Maryland. Frederick County's enslaved population had to wait until November 1, 1864, when they were emancipated under the new Maryland state constitution, which abolished slavery.

Slaves did a variety of jobs in Frederick County, just as they did across the United States before the Civil War. Among the most common slave occupations was unskilled farm labor, which included planting, weeding, and harvesting crops, tending to animals, and driving carriages. The common use of slaves on Frederick County farms was reflected by advertisements that ran in regional newspapers advertising agricultural goods for sale, which included "good farm hands." Other slaves performed skilled labor, typically male slaves trained in their masters' trades. This included blacksmithing, shoemaking, and mill operating. Sebastian "Boss" Hammond was one such enslaved man. His owners, Arianna Hammond and John Walker—and Colonel Thomas Hammond after John's death, allowed Boss to develop his skills as a stone carver and to earn money from this occupation. In 1839, Boss used seven hundred dollars he had saved to purchase his own freedom, eventually purchasing his wife and their five children. He was particularly renowned for the tombstones he produced, which are known for their singular beauty and can still be found throughout Frederick and Carroll Counties in the twenty-first century. Female slaves often performed agricultural duties, such as tending small livestock and maintaining gardens, as well as being used for household chores and to watch children. Civil War-era diarist Catherine Markell highlighted this aspect of slavery in 1858, describing her cousin's relationship with his slave Mary, noting that he "never took off his own shoes and stockings until tonight—his mammy Mary always waiting on him." Slaves were also hired out to others for temporary labor, often to farms for seasonal tasks. As a result, it was not uncommon in Frederick County to see slaves forced to labor for people who did not own them. The wage for this labor was collected by their master from the temporary employer and the slave sometimes received a portion of this fee. Frederick County newspapers often contained ads that sought temporary enslaved workers, such as one that asked for "a middle aged slave woman from the country, by the month or year, to cook wash and iron for a small family." One 1807 runaway slave ad placed by Elizabeth Luckett, who lived on Bentz Street in Frederick, illustrated this type of labor. She sought her slave Jack, whom she described as a joiner who had been rented out to John Brien at Antietam Mills.

✧ *Boss Hammond's stonework was particularly renowned and many other Frederick residents and businesses followed in his profession. This image shows the interior of U. A. Lough and Son Monumental Stoneworks.*

Most slave owners in Frederick County throughout the eighteenth and nineteenth centuries were farmers, but a broad range of other people also owned slaves, including professionals such as bankers, lawyers, and ministers. Most masters owned between one and four slaves, but some Frederick County residents held larger numbers. In the early nineteenth century, the county's two largest slave holders each owned approximately one hundred people. One was Victoire Vincendiére, who owned the plantation L'Hermitage, which is now part of the Monocacy National Battlefield Park, and the other was Thomas Sim Lee, who operated Needwood near Burkittsville. While Frederick County's slave population was relatively low compared to other Southern states, this did not necessarily mean that everyone who did not own slaves was against slavery. One Middletown man who did not own slaves stated "if [I found] a negro runaway I was in duty bound to catch him as if a horse or anything else had runaway." Even churches took positions on the issue. The leadership of Urbana's Methodist Church noted in their church's deed that "no abolitionist, or any person or persons belonging to or advocating the Abolition Doctrine shall have any control over management in said church, nor shall any minister, preacher or other person holding to or advocating said Abolition Doctrine be permitted at any time to preach or lecture in said church." As these examples demonstrate, slavery was an everyday institution in Frederick County and county residents held firm positions on the issue.

During the nineteenth century, just as the lives and experiences of slave owners and non-slave owners varied widely, so too were slaves' experiences diverse. The stories of individual slaves not only place a face on this dehumanizing social practice, but also let us appreciate the challenges they faced and the wide range of strategies they used to survive slavery. Hester Diggs was owned by Dr. John Baltzell's family, and her life illustrates the challenges to enslaved families. Not only was Hester owned by the Baltzells, but they also owned her three children, John Thomas, Ann, and Emma. In 1854, when Hester was thirty-seven, John Baltzell died and she was emancipated by his widow Ruth. However, Ruth did not release Hester's children, so after her emancipation Hester continued to live in Frederick with her husband, John. Emma was freed four years later, but John Thomas was sold to a man named John Williams. Hester was not reunited with her son until she moved to Cayuga County, New York, in 1869 after her husband's death. Hester lived a long life, well into her eighties, and, after outliving her husband, spent the rest of her life living in her daughter's home.

Earlier in the nineteenth century, the story of Catherine Hammond and Henry "Harry" Jones shows how relationships developed between slaves. Catherine and Harry were owned by the glove maker John Caspar Fritchie and his wife Barbara, who became famous during the Civil War. Catherine, who was the granddaughter of a free man named William Hammond, helped Barbara with housework while Harry assisted John in his craft. On December 6, 1827, Catherine and Harry married at the home of Mary Boone on Patrick Street. Reverend John Jones of All Saints Episcopal Church, where Harry was a member, officiated during the ceremony. After their marriage, their lives as slaves continued as before, until Catherine's death in May 1837. She was thirty-seven when she died, having never known freedom.

The story of Daniel Thompson, a slave owned by James Pearce in Liberty, illustrates the different paths slaves took to freedom during the Civil War. In 1863, with the war raging, Pearce emancipated Daniel. He did this so that Daniel could fight for the Union against slavery, the very institution Pearce practiced, which was the central cause of the war. On August 4, 1863, Daniel enlisted in the Fourth Regiment of the U.S. Colored Infantry as a free man. His military service took him throughout Maryland, North Carolina, and Virginia, and he participated in

✧ *While still enslaved, Laura Frazier is pictured here with Nannie and William Tyler Page.*

actions at Bermuda Hundred, Petersburg, Dutch Gap, Chapin's Farm, and Fort Fisher. He left the army on May 4, 1866, having achieved the rank of corporal.

For many slaves, the exit from slavery posed its own difficulties. Laura Frazier was born in 1851 and was the fifth daughter in her family. Her mother had been a slave for over forty years. Laura remained enslaved until after the Civil War, when Maryland's new state constitution abolished slavery. At this time, she was a slave of Frederick's Page family and, following emancipation, Laura stayed in Frederick with her mother and two nieces in Kleinhart's Alley. Laura remained as a paid domestic servant working for her previous owners, the Tyler family. As a free woman, Laura married William Downs, who worked at the Maryland School for the Deaf. Laura and William did not have children, but they were very active in community organizations throughout their lives. William was a member of Fredericktonian Lodge of Prince Hall, a national organization of African-American Freemasons, and he and Laura were members of Queen Esther Chapter of the Eastern Star, a Masonic auxiliary organization.

As a consideration of slavery shows, farming was important in Frederick County. However, it was far from the only way to make a living in the nineteenth century. Many craftspeople produced their wares throughout the county. While it is unclear when pottery began to be produced in the region, many potters were clustered around Frederick and Thurmont, and many of these potters were of German descent. One large pottery shop, Lynn Pottery, was opened in Frederick by Jacob Lynn in 1845. Another important group of craftspeople in Frederick County were furniture makers, who were well-known throughout pre-revolutionary America for their products. Many furniture makers in western Maryland were German, and their style reflected their heritage: their products were stockier and less delicate than the wares produced by English craftspeople around Baltimore. Prominent furniture makers in the county included James Whitehill, who worked in Libertytown in 1822 before moving to Frederick in 1829, and Wolfville's Christopher Columbus Stottlemyer. Many furniture makers also doubled as undertakers, producing both coffins and furniture. This included the Carty family of Frederick, the Creager family of Thurmont, and the Gladhill family of Middletown.

Pottery and furniture were necessities, but area craftspeople also produced luxury items, particularly silver goods and fine clocks, and, as with the potters and furniture makers, many of these artisans were German. These luxury goods artisans became particularly prominent following the revolution and continued working into the mid-1800s. One well-known clockmaker and silversmith, John Fessler, emigrated to America from Switzerland in 1771. He supported the Continental Congress and served in the Continental Army before settling in Frederick in 1782. His descendants maintained his business until 1917. A contemporary of Fessler's, Frederick Augustis Heisley, born in Lancaster, Pennsylvania, also served in the Continental Army and operated in Frederick from 1783 to 1816. These two men knew each other well. They collaborated to create the works for the town clock housed in the German Church Steeple and socialized in the same circles. Both served as vestrymen for the Lutheran Church.

Frederick County's natural resources enabled other forms of artisanal crafts. The county's geology—which included sands with a high silica content, clays, and abundant timber—led to glass production in Frederick County as early as 1775. Around this time, a factory was built near the Monocacy River on Big Bennett Creek. The largest and most well-known glass manufacturer in the county, New Bremen, also operated on Big Bennett. It was originally an industrial plantation founded by John Frederick Amelung, a German-born glassmaker from Bremen. Amelung funded his operation with German and American investors, including Thomas Johnson and Charles Carroll, who had been sent letters by John Adams and Benjamin Franklin on Amelung's behalf. By 1785, New Bremen had a blacksmith, a tailor, a shoemaker, a sawmill, and a school that taught both English and German. There were also thirty houses, where both free and slave workers lived. In 1787, Amelung returned to his roots and began to produce glass, an operation that expanded to include a second glass house and over four hundred workers by 1790, along with warehouses in Philadelphia, New York City, Baltimore, and Frederick. Amelung also carefully courted prominent people and made presentation pieces for politicians, which likely helped him secure additional money in 1788 to fund his expansion. However, many American consumers found New Bremen's glass to be stylistically old fashioned and this combined with high transportation costs to impede Amelung's enterprise. Following a

✧ *John Fessler and his wife.*

pair of fires in 1790 at New Bremen and one of the glass factories, the New Bremen Glass Manufactory closed in 1794 and, along with it, the high mark of glass production in Maryland ended as well. Some glass making continued into the nineteenth century, but it never again reached the heights that Amelung's business briefly attained.

Another major occupation in Frederick County grew out of a local cottage industry. In the 1700s, the processing of wool into cloth became established in the region. Carding mills made raw wool ready for spinning, and fulling mills cleaned and shrank woven wool cloth for strength. These mills worked on order for individual customers. By 1811 eleven fulling mills were processing forty-four thousand yards of cloth and nine carding mills were working over thirty-five thousand pounds of wool. International events helped the local industry, as the Embargo of 1809 slowed cloth importation and the War of 1812 stopped it entirely. These were likely major reasons that Solomon Shepherd, the owner of an older fulling mill near Union Bridge, expanded his operations in 1810 to include carding, spinning, and weaving. This situation was only temporary. After the war, a flood of European textiles entered the United States, but numerous textile mills continued operating throughout the county during the first half of the nineteenth century. One was the Fleecy Dale woolen mill, opened on the site of the old Amelung glass factory, where by 1820 fourteen women, ten men, and fifteen children worked. Other factories included Union Woolen—near Jefferson—and Mechanicstown Woolen, both of which were operating by 1835.

Along with artisanal workshops and the region's many mills, other industrial producers tapped into the county's mineral resources. Large and long-lasting iron producers were a major industrial presence in the county before and after the revolution. These iron furnaces used natural resources in the region other than only iron ore. At the average eighteenth century iron furnace most of the work went into harvesting timber to produce charcoal, which was used to produce molten iron ore. This molten ore was then fluxed with limestone to remove impurities. The molten iron was run into sand trenches, called sows and pigs, from which pig iron, a brittle initial product, derives its name. The pig iron was then worked by hammers, typically at on-site forges, into more malleable and usable iron bars. This industry had its origin under the Maryland colonial government to meet a British need for iron, which was caused by the shortage of timber in Britain. During the early nineteenth century, Frederick County iron works relied on slave labor, due to the extensive manpower requirements and the availability of slaves with knowledge of the industry. This came from an extensive iron industry in West Africa, which gave many African men sold into slavery experience in iron production. As the nineteenth century continued, the iron industry declined in Frederick County due to increasingly depleted timber resources and growing competition from the Lake Superior region, Alabama, England, Sweden, and Russia.

✧ *An example of Amelung glass. This piece is decorated with symbols of Freemasonry, such as the square and compass. Masonry, with its emphasis on moral development and reciprocity, was an important social outlet in the new American republic.*

One major Frederick County iron works epitomized the trajectory of the iron industry. In 1767, the Johnson brothers, members of the landed gentry, sold Hampton Furnace—west of what is now Emmitsburg—and constructed Catoctin Furnace on Little Hunting Creek in 1744. During the revolution they produced cast shell, shot, dutch ovens, and other camping equipment for the Continental Army. In 1800, two brothers, Thomas and Baker Johnson, began operating the facility. Thomas sold his equity to Baker in 1802, and the furnace was sold outside the family with Baker's death in 1811. Catoctin Furnace used slave labor, which peaked with twenty slaves in 1830. This number declined by 1841 as the furnace's operators realized that housing and feeding slaves was more expensive than paying free white workers a wage. The 1860 census listed the furnace's value at one hundred thousand dollars, when it employed ninety men and used an eighty-horsepower steam engine to produce 4,500 tons of pig iron a year. Following the Civil

✧ *Catoctin Furnace at the height of its productivity, c. 1875.*

✧ *Although later eclipsed by the railroad, the C&O Canal was a major route for trade in the emergent American republic. This is Lock 30 near Brunswick, Maryland.*

COURTESY OF THE BRUNSWICK MUSEUM.

War, this output increased and in 1873 operator Jacob M. Kunkel built a new steam-powered, hot-blast, coke-burning furnace—nicknamed "Deborah"—which produced thirty-five tons of pig iron a day. Catoctin Furnace's output peaked in the 1880s, when it produced twelve-thousand tons of pig iron a year and employed five hundred men. However, Catoctin Furnace faced the same difficulties other regional iron furnaces faced and Joseph E. Thropp of Earlston, Pennsylvania, purchased the failing facility in 1905. After seeing the furnace through bankruptcy court, Thropp continued to mine iron from the acreage, but shipped the ore to his furnace in Pennsylvania for production.

During this period, western Maryland helped bridge the expanding U.S. westward frontier with the nation's urban centers on the Atlantic Seaboard. In 1804, the Maryland State Legislature incorporated three turnpike companies to begin the National Road, a major transportation project stretching from Baltimore to Cumberland. Eventually, the road continued west, crossing the Ohio River at Wheeling, Virginia, and ending at Vandalia, Illinois. Two competing westward transportation routes were established two decades later along the same general route. On July 4, 1828, both the Chesapeake and Ohio Canal and the Baltimore and Ohio Railroad broke ground, which started a race to become the dominant freight route to the west. Rooted in a series of locks and canals that George Washington had established with early iron makers, such as Thomas Johnson, in the 1750s and 1780s, the Potowmak Canal Company was already a focus of regional transportation networks. With this success, the C&O Canal was designed to link this regional network—largely grounded along the Potomac River—to the Ohio River. Also paralleling the Potomac River was the B&O Railroad, which was planned to stretch from Baltimore to Wheeling. The B&O was not the only railroad in western Maryland. A variety of regional railroad companies also worked to connect to broader networks. These networks hurt home manufacturing as residents could more easily purchase goods, but enabled industrial expansion later in the nineteenth century, particularly following the Civil War. Although the C&O Canal remained an important trade route for over one hundred years, the railroad extended faster and ultimately overtook the water route as the primary passage for goods traveling west.

Alongside increasing production and transportation during this period, Frederick County also developed its educational system—first for those wealthy enough to afford it and later for the broader population. Before the revolution, regional schools were small, one-room schoolhouses scattered throughout the county. These were private schools, but those who could afford to do so typically hired private tutors. People entering trades worked under masters as apprentices, exchanging labor for training, rather than taking formal classes. The Maryland colonial government mandated schools in 1723 requiring each county to maintain a school near the center of the county, although this law was laxly enforced. Many early schools were linked to churches or religious personnel, such as Needwood Forest near Petersville, which was a school for boys operated by the Reverend Bartholomew Booth. The sons of many prominent persons—including Benedict Arnold, General Charles Lee, and Mrs. Hannah Washington—attended Needwood Forest.

✧ *A group of men, likely composed of employees and some executives, in front of a brick kiln, c. 1880.*

One early county public school was the Frederick Free School, which was chartered in 1763 and received funding from the state tax system. Other public schools were established following the revolution. Thurmont constructed its first public school in 1796. Lotteries were held to build public schools in other communities, including Emmitsburg in 1808, Middletown in 1809, and Taneytown in 1815. This process was formalized and, in 1816, a new state law was passed requiring each county to invest until they could provide a free, public school in each district. A new infrastructure developed to manage this system, including requirements that teachers pass examinations for teaching certificates, that a school tax be established, and that state superintendents, school commissioners, and inspectors be appointed. With this system in place, Jefferson's "Union" school opened in 1824. It was replaced by a two-room schoolhouse in 1841, and a second story was added in 1861. This building served Jefferson until 1924, when the structure was razed during the construction of a new school. To increase access to public educations, the Levy Court of Frederick County ruled in 1837 that funds should be levied to allow all white children between five and eighteen years old to get public educations. Even with this system in place, most children did not remain in school beyond twelve years old. The following year, the state legislature permitted the establishment of separate schools for women. With the rapid development of public education in Maryland, roughly ten thousand Frederick County children were enrolled in public schools by 1846.

While Frederick County's public school system developed, the region continued to house a thriving private education system. These schools often kept their students separate from their wider communities. Some went to elaborate lengths to do this. Visitation Academy, a Catholic girls' school in Frederick, required parents to provide lists of people with whom their daughters could correspond—lists the school asked be kept short. An order of nuns, the Sisters of the Visitation, founded the school in 1846 as the Academy of the Visitation. The building's central section—constructed in the mid-1820s—had been used by the Sisters of Charity as a school for disadvantaged and orphaned children. When Jesuit priests decided to open a girls' boarding school at the location, the Sisters of Charity left. The curricula at Visitation Academy trained students in the natural and philosophical sciences, along with more traditional women's coursework. This additional training may explain the disproportionate number of female professionals and community leaders produced by Visitation throughout its history. One was Mary Lee Smith née Palmer, a Visitation student during the Civil War, who was a founder of the Historical Society of Frederick County. The school remains a central part of downtown Frederick in the early twenty-first century, although it was taken over by a private organization after the remaining three Sisters of the Visitation were moved to Richmond, Virginia, in 2005. Other private religious women's schools included the Frederick Female Seminary, opened in 1843 by Hiram Winchester to foster "the promotion and advancement of female education and the cultivation and diffusion of literature and science," and St John's Female Benevolent School, which was founded in Frederick by five Sisters of Charity from Emmitsburg in 1824.

✧ *A group of Visitation Academy Students, c. 1915.*

✧ *Hiram Winchester.*

Colleges also began to develop in Frederick County after the revolution. They were often linked to the county's religious institutions. In 1793, Aloysius Elder sold a parcel of land to John Carroll to establish a church for English Catholics near Emmitsburg. At the same time, James Hughes built St. Joseph's Church in Emmitsburg to serve an Irish Catholic congregation. In 1805, John DuBois, a French priest who became Frederick's

✧ *The interior of the Elizabeth Seton Shrine.*

pastor in 1794, laid the cornerstone of Saint-Mary-on-the-Hill, uniting Emmitsburg's Irish and English congregations and establishing the foundation for Mount Saint Mary's Seminary, an all-male religious school. DuBois became the Mount's first president in 1808, and in 1809 he housed Elizabeth Ann Seton and a group of young women, who had arrived in Emmitsburg to found a school. This led to a long-standing relationship between the Mount and Seton's school. Some seminary graduates went on to establish other Catholic colleges in the United States during the mid-nineteenth century. Others held high religious offices in the Catholic Church, such as John Hughes, who was named the first archbishop of New York in 1842. The Mount was involved in major political and social movements of the period, including the decision by the Mount's president and council to free the college's last slave in 1858, only a few years before the Civil War began. Mount Saint Mary's began admitting women in 1972 and achieved university status in 2004.

Frederick County was also home to many professionals, such as lawyers and doctors, some of whom became nationally famous in the new republic. Many aspiring lawyers started their practices in Frederick during this period. One such lawyer was Roger Brooke Taney, who opened a law practice in Frederick in 1801. He viewed this as the most profitable place to practice, following Annapolis and Baltimore. Originally from Calvert County, Maryland, Taney attended Dickenson College in Carlisle, Pennsylvania. After college, he studied law in Annapolis and, after moving to Frederick, found some of his fellow students practicing in Frederick, including another famous Frederick lawyer, Francis Scott Key. Taney and Key had both studied under Jeremiah Townley Chase, and moved in the same social circles; in fact, Taney married Key's sister Anne. Taney's early legal career dealt with land and property disputes, debt collections, and civil suits. He represented many business clients in Frederick and was active in Frederick's schools, serving on the Board of Visitors for Frederick Academy and attending school examinations for the Frederick Female Seminary. He mentored several law clerks and other budding lawyers. Taney lived in Frederick for almost twenty-two years, before moving to Baltimore. He went on to serve both Maryland and the United States as an attorney general and, most famously, as a Supreme Court chief justice. While on the Supreme Court, he served as chief justice for one of the most infamous decisions in American history: the Dred Scott decision. Scott, a slave, sued to be free following unsuccessful attempts to purchase his and his family's freedom from his previous master's widow. The core of his case was that, having lived in two free territories, Illinois and Wisconsin, he and his family should be emancipated. Similar cases had emancipated slaves in the past and this was expected to be a relatively simple decision. However, the initial case was thrown out on a technicality and the Supreme Court of Missouri reversed decades of decisions by finding for his owner. Now owned by his previous owner's brother, Scott sued in federal court, eventually appealing to the U.S. Supreme Court. Scott's suit was rejected by a six-to-three decision and he was forced to remain a slave. Taney wrote the majority opinion, handed down in March 1857, arguing that Scott was not a U.S. citizen and so not eligible to sue in federal court. Not only did Taney suggest that

✧ *Roger Brooke Taney.*

slaves were not U.S. citizens, but that any person of African descent, free or slave, could not hold American citizenship. Taney argued that blacks had been viewed by the U.S. Constitution's authors as "beings of an inferior order, and altogether unfit to associate with the white race." This racial argument was challenged by the dissenting court justices, who found no historical basis for Taney's position because the Constitution's authors did not object to antislavery provisions in the Northwest Ordinance and that blacks could vote in five of the initial thirteen states. Taney also suggested that freeing Scott would violate his owner's Fifth Amendment rights by depriving him of his property. Taney's decision not only reproduced unsubstantiated claims about racial capability that justified slavery, but also enabled slave owners to freely bring slaves into free states and territories, deepening the divisions over slavery that erupted into the American Civil War.

Taney's brother-in-law, Francis Scott Key, was another celebrated Frederick lawyer, but his fame was not a direct result of his legal career. Key was born in what was then Frederick County, although the location of his birth is now part of Carroll County. He followed his father and uncle into the legal field. After studying law, Key briefly practiced in Frederick before moving to Georgetown after his marriage in 1802, where he worked with his uncle. By the War of 1812, in which he achieved fame for penning *The Star Spangled Banner* as described on page 25, Key was an established lawyer in Georgetown.

✧ *Francis Scott Key's boyhood home, Terra Rubra, attracted tourists in the late nineteenth century. Photographed at the springhouse, c. 1900, this couple dressed in their best clothes to visit this landmark.*

✧ *Francis Scott Key.*

A famous Frederick doctor was John Baltzell, who was born in Frederick in 1775 to John Jacob and Ann Maria Baltzell, early county settlers. John Jacob's mother was the sister of early European settler Margaret Schley. John studied medicine under Philip Thomas and went on to a prominent medical career. He was appointed surgeon's mate on September 3, 1799, and later was named surgeon of the Maryland Regiment on February 14, 1815. When he was forty-one, John married Ruth Ridgely, a twenty-two year old from Baltimore, and the couple became the first owners of the Church Street house that became the headquarters of the Historical Society of Frederick County in 1959.

Alongside schools, churches, and workplaces, community was also formed in such social spaces as colonial taverns, where local people gathered, and travelers obtained lodging and meals. People learned news from around the region and across the nation in taverns, and also formed relationships in them. According to local legend, John Ross Key met and courted his future wife Anne Charlton in her parent's tavern. This couple were Francis Scott Key's parents. Catherine Kimball's tavern in Frederick illustrates the importance of taverns in the colonial period. During a brief visit to Frederick in 1791, President George Washington visited the establishment. Although he stayed at Brother's Tavern, Kimball's was better for public entertainment. Local diarist Jacob Engelbrecht described this entertainment on January 29, 1828: "Mr. Nichols (of Nantucket Massachusetts) the ventriloquist is at present in town & has performed for 3 nights to crowded audiences at Mrs. Kimball's hotel. Admittance 50 cents. I was not there." In a letter on April 11, 1821, Roger Brooke Taney described her tavern as "the only good boarding house in this town." Another prominent nineteenth-century tavern was the Old Stone Tavern on the southwest corner of Telegraph and West Patrick Streets run by Mr. Bowers. Many famous people stayed there, including Henry Clay, Andrew Jackson, and Daniel Webster. It was also the subject of a poem by Folger McKinsey, the editor of the *Frederick News* in the late nineteenth century, who was known as the Bentztown Bard.

Taverns were also central meeting places for a prominent aspect of post-Revolutionary male sociality: fraternal organizations. These civic organizations, of which Freemasonry remains the largest and most prominent example, often had closed meetings in taverns or members' homes before they established a dedicated lodge building. At least two lodges formed in Frederick County before the 1799 chartering of Hiram Lodge 28, which was the first clearly recognized Masonic lodge in the area. One early lodge met in 1790 in an Urbana house kept as a tavern and may have been organized by John Frederick Amelung. The longest-lasting lodge in Frederick County has been Columbia Lodge 58, which was chartered in 1815 and continues to meet in the early twenty-first century. Two prominent early lodge members owned taverns. Captain James Neale operated the Sign of the Spread Eagle, which he purchased from Major Henry Brother, on Patrick Street before 1800. The location of the Sign of the Spread Eagle later became the Central Hotel. In his diary for August 5, 1826, Jacob Engelbrecht notes "M. E. Bartgis Esquire tavern keeper Corner of Church and Court Streets this day raised a new sign painted by William V. Morgan. The design is A Masonic Emblem with the 'Central Hotel' in letters above and below." During this period, Masonry was prestigious and businessmen frequently displayed its regalia on signs to show their membership and to attract customers.

✧ *Peter's Tavern, on the "Lost and Found" parcel, was owned by John and Ruth Peters.*

While taverns provided everyday social outlets, large annual agricultural fairs provided opportunities for spectacle, relaxation, and commerce. These events originated under British colonial rule and continued as major annual regional events. Such fairs began in the 1700s

✧ *Livery stables boarded or rented horses and were necessary in American communities from the colonial period through the early twentieth century. Myers Livery Stable was owned by George Edward Myers who bought it in 1901 and operated it in Locust Alley in Frederick until 1909.*

✧ *Daniel Dulany the Elder (1685–1753), a prominent lawyer and member of the Maryland General Assembly before the revolution, became a land developer in the 1720s and is credited with the founding of Frederick.*

throughout Britain and its colonies as agricultural societies sponsored by the wealthy and influential, including English gentleman farmers and the Crown. These societies promulgated new agricultural technologies and were promoted by important individuals, including George Washington, Thomas Jefferson, and James Madison. In Frederick County, Daniel Dulany held a fair near Frederick as early as 1747. The fair was biannual, with each instance held over three days starting on May 10 and October 21, respectively. He also held a market on each Saturday in November. Any county resident could sell goods, including livestock and produce, at these fairs without paying an exhibition fee for five years. Aside from Dulaney's fairs, agricultural societies were active in the region in the nineteenth century. The Frederick County Agricultural Society held an annual cattle show and fair starting in 1822 at locations including Guy Creager's tavern near the Monocacy Bridge and Mrs. Cookerly's tavern near Libertytown. The longest-running fair began in 1853, when the Agricultural Society of Frederick County held the Great Frederick Fair for three days starting on October 12 at the old Hessian Barracks. County residents—among them Margaret Scholl Hood, who recorded the event in her diary—were impressed by the variety of goods and produce available.

THE WAR OF 1812

The War of 1812 disrupted Frederick County in the early nineteenth century and saw many county residents swept up in a new conflict with England. Although isolationist impulses existed in the new republic—George Washington had warned about the dangers of foreign affairs in his final speech as president in 1796—this proved difficult to maintain. Slightly more than a decade later, international entanglements became hard to avoid as hostilities between England and France heated up during the Napoleonic Wars. During this conflict, the British navy harassed American merchant ships and press-ganged sailors, while American Indian nations received British assistance in territorial struggles in the west. One incident directly involved a Frederick County man. On June 22, 1807, a short battle erupted between a U.S. ship, the *Chesapeake*, and a British ship, the *Leopard*, off of Norfolk, Virginia, when the *Chesapeake*'s captain refused to allow the *Leopard*'s crew to board. After the *Chesapeake*'s surrender, the *Leopard* took four members of the *Chesapeake*'s crew prisoner, who they believed to be British deserters. One, William Ware, was from Pine Creek in Frederick County. One man was hanged and the other three, including Ware, were sentenced to five years of British naval service. This incident outraged the U.S. public and led to an embargo against British trade. The *Frederick Town Herald* described the event this way:

> To the Citizens of Frederick-town and its vicinity: The late outrage committed by a British squadron on a vessel of the United States, calls for all your indignation, and all your energy. The long chain of insults, murders and robberies, which we have suffered from the British government, ought to end here. As an event of such serious importance, and so degrading to our character as a "free and independent" people, requires an expression of the public sentiment.

This was not an isolated incident. By 1808, more than four thousand American sailors were impressed by the British and less than a thousand were returned. In this context, the Maryland legislature passed acts organizing and strengthening the state militia. These acts required all white men between the ages of eighteen and forty-five to perform military service, with the exception of professionals such as government officers, doctors, professors, ferry pilots, and sailors.

Given these tensions, the United States declared war on England, beginning the War of 1812, a conflict that saw the burning of the new capital, Washington, D.C., and increased solidarity among the American states. Early in the conflict the British isolated the American states. In 1813, British ships blockaded prominent ports on the U.S. eastern seaboard, damaging trade and preventing easy travel between states or to Europe. With this threat to the republic, Frederick County men again joined the militias. Recruiting officers offered volunteers sixteen dollars upon enlistment with a five dollar salary a month, as well as 160 acres of land. Between required militia service in Maryland, the fiscal benefits of military service, and patriotic sentiment, officials worried that there would not be enough workers to maintain Frederick County's agricultural output. Militia officers often tried to keep their soldiers home during the busiest part of the agricultural calendar. Annapolis' General Winder wrote to Colonel Henry Stembel of Middletown in 1814, noting "It is but recently we have had occasion to call into service any part of the militia; and being desirous as much as possible to avoid calling them a great distance from home until the harvest was gathered in."

Other officers worked to increase the military's size as the war intensified. In the Battle of Bladensburg, the British defeated American forces and burned Washington, D.C., in August 1814. After hearing of the coming battle, Captain John Brengle and Reverend David Schaeffer spent four hours in the streets of Frederick, calling for recruits to defend Washington, D.C., as the British approached. They raised a company of eighty men and left to defend the capital. However, upon reaching Clarksburg, the group learned that the American forces had already lost at Bladensburg. They were sent to Baltimore, where they were joined by other Frederick County companies. All of these Frederick County men saw action during the Battle of Baltimore, in which American and British forces fought on land and sea. The British commander, Major General Robert Ross, was killed in initial fighting at North Point, an engagement that delayed the British and gave the American defenders time to prepare. The British were then halted at Hampstead Hill, which was more strongly fortified than anticipated, as the defenders of Fort McHenry weathered a massive British naval bombardment. The British loss at Baltimore turned the tide of the war and marked the penultimate major attack on the United States by the British in the conflict.

Militia members were not the only Frederick County men present at the Battle of Baltimore. Georgetown lawyer and Frederick County native Francis Scott Key observed the British bombardment and immortalized the events in a poem that became the U.S. national anthem. Following the burning of Washington, D.C., the British captured Dr. William Beans, a physician in Upper Marlboro. Before the battle of Bladensburg, Beans hosted British officers in his home, but, with other Upper Marlboro citizens, seized straggling British troops returning to their ships after the burning of the capital. Surprised by his actions, British officers sent troops to capture the doctor. An American delegation was sent to negotiate for Beans's release, as he was not a young man and—if taken to Canada as a British prisoner—he might not live long enough to return home. Francis Scott Key joined this delegation, which was headed by experienced negotiator Colonel John Skinner. Key and Skinner approached the British royal navy under a flag of truce on September 5. Upon hearing of the safe treatment of British prisoners by American forces, the British agreed to release Beans. With the attack on Baltimore imminent, British troops held Key, Skinner, and Beans on the delegation's small ship. From this vantage point, they observed the Battle of Baltimore, including the twenty-four hour bombardment of Fort McHenry. Watching from eight miles away, they could not be sure of the result of the fierce attack and shelling throughout the night. Shortly before dawn, the fighting ended and the men eagerly watched for any sign of which side had won. With the dawn, they saw the American flag flying over the fort and knew the British had lost. Inspired and excited by the American victory, Key, an amateur poet, commemor ated the event in a poem titled *Defense of Fort McHenry*. Later, the poem was set to the tune of a popular drinking song, *To Anacreon in Heaven*, and renamed *The Star Spangled Banner*. Following a swell in popularity during the Civil War, the song rose to national prominence and became the U.S. national anthem in 1931.

With its proximity to major events in the War of 1812, civilians and military forces stored valuable people and objects in Frederick. As in the Revolutionary War, British prisoners were held at the Frederick Town Barracks by local militia. After the Battle of Bladensburg, over one hundred British prisoners were marched to the barracks from Washington, D.C. Civilians stored valuables in Frederick, particularly as the British military operated throughout the Chesapeake Bay region in 1814. For example Roger Brooke Taney's mother, Monica Taney, left the family's Calvert County estate to take refuge with her son in Frederick. The secretaries of War and the Treasury fled to Frederick with important public papers when the British captured and burned Washington, D.C. Businesses also took this precaution, among them the Farmer's Bank of Maryland, which closed its Annapolis branch and operated exclusively out of its Frederick branch. The proximity to the conflict that made it easy to take refuge in Frederick County was also a concern, as some citizens feared that the British would send a detachment to seize the money and other valuables stored in Frederick. It would be a short trip for British forces to advance from Frederick to Harper's Ferry and destroy the federal armory there.

Even during the fighting throughout the Chesapeake region, both sides were negotiating to end the conflict. Peace negotiations began in 1814, with England pushing for both sides to retain their new borders and for the United States to cede the Northwest Territory, roughly from Ohio to Wisconsin, to the British's American Indian allies. However, negotiations were slow and the final version of the treaty was much different than that proposed by the British. The treaty was signed on December 24, 1814. It returned all British and American territories to their pre-war boundaries and assured American Indian nations that their possessions and rights as of 1811 would be retained. As there were few firm details on tribal borders, this clause offered few protections to American Indians, particularly after Shawnee leader Tecumseh's death and a string of British military losses. While British and American boundaries remained the same after this conflict, the war solidified a more unified sense of American political and national identity.

Ten years after the War of 1812's end, Frederick residents remembered the American Revolution in high style. One of the war's heroes, Gilbert du Motier—the famed Marquis de Lafayette—accepted a formal invitation from President James Monroe to commemorate the fiftieth anniversary of the revolution with a tour of the United States. Lafayette was a major-general under Washington and fought in many key battles during the revolution. This tour encompassed all twenty-four existing states, including large cities such as Boston and Philadelphia. During his tour, Lafayette was invited to Frederick by Colonel McPherson and made a grand entrance into the city at four o'clock in the

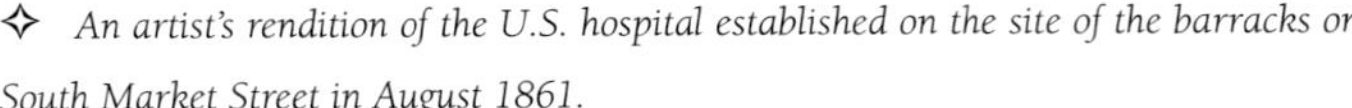

✧ *An artist's rendition of the U.S. hospital established on the site of the barracks on South Market Street in August 1861.*

✧ *The Jug Bridge and the memorial commemorating the Marquis de Lafayette's visit, c. 1910.*

afternoon on December 29, 1824. He travelled down the National Road and met a welcoming committee after crossing the Jug Bridge. The committee was made up of prominent citizens, including local congressmen, Dr. John Baltzell, Colonel John Ritchie, and Judge Abraham Shriver. Lafayette gave a short speech, noting "after having been forty years ago adopted [as a citizen] by a peculiar vote of the State of Maryland, I think myself doubly happy, Sir, to be most kindly welcomed by the citizens of Frederick County." The marquis's entourage paraded along South Market Street, where, according to Engelbrecht, seven to eight thousand people watched the parade, over half of whom were not Frederick citizens. The city greeted him with gun shots, trumpets, church bells, and decorative arches erected across important streets. The parade ended on Court Square at McPherson's home—known as the McPherson-Ross House in the early twenty-first century—where he stayed during his visit to Frederick. On December 30, a ball—which newspapers called Frederick's greatest social affair—was held at Joseph Talbott's hotel in the marquis's honor. For five dollars, men could buy one of two hundred available tickets, while women needed formal invitations to the ball. A band opened the affair with Francis Johnson's *General Lafayette's March*, and attendees honored the revolutionary icon with music, dancing, and dining throughout the evening. For these few days in the early nineteenth century, Frederick County was at the center of public spectacle in the United States, celebrating the first fifty years of the revolutionary experiment. Within the next fifty years, Frederick County bore witness to events that threatened to tear the young republic apart.

CIVIL WAR AND POST-CIVIL WAR LIFE

As residents of a border state, Frederick County's inhabitants experienced the chaos and violence of the American Civil War. The battles of South Mountain and Monocacy were fought in Frederick County and two of the war's seminal battles—Antietam and Gettysburg—occurred in neighboring counties, so Frederick County's citizens saw the toll of war firsthand. The Baltimore and Ohio Railroad and the National Road were used by both armies. These routes were oriented east-west through western Maryland, economically linking the region to cities like Baltimore and Washington, D.C. This likely contributed to the state's decision to remain with the North, although many Marylanders favored the South. Frederick County's residents, whether loyal to the Union or sympathetic to the Confederacy, faced many challenges during the war. After the Battle of Antietam, the city was used as a station for wounded soldiers, echoing the aftermath of Braddock's 1755 campaign. This time, wounded and dying men were so widespread that a commentator described Frederick as "one vast hospital." Throughout its churches, schools, and other public buildings, trained physicians and local volunteers struggled to save lives.

While violence between abolitionists and pro-slavery forces had erupted before, John Brown's raid on Harpers Ferry, Virginia, in 1859 marked a crucial moment in the build-up to the Civil War. Brown, an abolitionist, had reached national infamy through his role in the series of raids and counter-raids in Kansas. He sought to seize the national armory at Harpers Ferry and use the munitions to fuel a slave revolt in the South. Brown and a band of raiders attacked on October 16. Although Brown's men seized key positions in Harpers Ferry, a train from Wheeling, Virginia, was stopped, but then allowed to continue on to Monocacy Depot where they alerted the authorities. Telegraphs spread the news throughout the county. On October 17, the Junior Defenders, the United Guards, and the Independent Riflemen—militia companies formed from Frederick's volunteer firefighters—

set out to retake the armory under Colonel Edward Shriver. These companies, along with others from Maryland and Virginia, guarded Harpers Ferry's perimeter while U.S. marines under Colonel Robert E. Lee stormed an engine house that Brown and his remaining men had fortified. Brown did not cause a large-scale slave rebellion, but he raised tensions over slavery throughout the North and the South. Ralph Waldo Emerson described Brown's hanging on December 2, 1859, as martyrdom, suggesting that Brown would "make the gallows glorious like the cross." In contrast, Colonel John Preston of the Virginia Military Institute said of the execution, "So perish all such enemies of Virginia." After the raid, Southern states began to expand state militias. With tensions building prior to Abraham Lincoln's inauguration in 1861, Southern secession erupted—beginning with South Carolina on December 20, 1861—and the Civil War began.

✧ *Union troops in Frederick during the Civil War.*

While Maryland remained loyal to the Union, its communities were deeply divided between Unionists and Confederates, particularly over the issue of slavery. With the Mason-Dixon Line dividing North and South forming its northern border, Maryland was a border state. Many of the state's residents hoped for a peaceful resolution to the war that would either maintain the Union or let the Confederacy secede. As the war began, opinion in Maryland generally split, with the east's coastal plantations and ports favoring the Confederacy and the west's towns and communities supporting the Union. Frederick County was no exception to this division. Given its position between eastern and western Maryland, opinion on the war divided Frederick County, with about two-thirds of Frederick's residents favoring the Union. In Frederick itself, this division is readily apparent within the writings of two diarists: Jacob Engelbrecht and Catherine Markell.

Early in the war, Engelbrecht recorded many pro-Union events in Frederick County. On January 21, 1861—upon receiving news of the secession of South Carolina, Mississippi, Alabama, and Florida—members of Frederick's Union Party erected a ninety-six-foot hickory Union Pole on the corner of Bentz and Fourth Street. On February 6, with tensions rising, Engelbrecht noted that:

> Today at 2 o'clock a Union flag was flung to the breeze from MacGill's to Keefer['s] 3 story houses [on the] corner of Patrick & Market Street. The American Band were there & after playing "Hail Columbia" the flag was drawn across to the centre of the street, after which, a glee club sung "*the Star Spangled Banner*"... On the flag was "The Nation must be preserved" Huzza! for the Union.

Others sympathized with the Confederacy. Catherine Markell—who lived near Engelbrecht—also kept a diary during the war. As a Confederate supporter, she presented a Southern perspective, often socializing with Confederate officers during their occupations of the city. Reproducing an image of the Southern forces as romantic, she described Confederate Major General J. E. B. Stuart as "a gay, rollicking cavalier and a great favorite with the girls." Her husband, Fred, shared her loyalties, and left Frederick for Hagerstown in the absence of Confederate forces.

With Southern states in open rebellion, Maryland was in a tenuous political position. The expectations that Maryland would pick a side became increasingly important with Virginia's secession on April 17. With a neighboring state in the Confederacy, violent incidents and political turmoil increased in Maryland. On April 19, a pro-Confederate mob attacked the Sixth Massachusetts Volunteer Infantry in Baltimore, leading tacitly pro-Union Maryland Governor Thomas Hicks to ask Lincoln to stop moving federal troops through the state. Lincoln refused, and Hicks used state militias to disable the railroads. On April 22, Hicks called the Maryland General Assembly into a special session. Due to pro-Confederate leanings in Annapolis—and its occupation by Union troops—Hicks brought the assembly to largely pro-Union Frederick. On April 26, the assembly discussed secession at the Frederick courthouse. Due to the building's small size, the session shifted to Kemp Hall on April 27. In Kemp Hall, the assembly wrote:

> We cannot but know that a large proportion of the citizens of Maryland have been induced to believe that our deliberations may result in the passage of some measure committing the State to secession. It is, therefore, our duty to declare that all such fears are without just foundation. We know that we have no constitutional authority to take such action. You need not fear that there is a possibility that we will do so.

With this statement, the Maryland General Assembly signaled the state's intention to remain with the Union. On the same day, in response to Hicks's closure of the railroads, President Lincoln took extreme action and suspended the writ of habeas corpus along the rail route from Philadelphia to Washington, D.C. In another session in Frederick that summer, state legislators brought a resolution calling for secession before the assembly. The bill failed and many legislators, even the pro-Southern delegates, echoed the assembly's previous statement: that Maryland did not have the constitutional authority to leave the Union. However, their activity was not completely pro-Union. The legislators refused to reopen rail lines to the North and issued a resolution to protest the federal occupation. The Maryland Assembly held a special vote on secession on July 15, 1861, which again showed a strong Union majority. This outcome virtually assured the impossibility of Maryland joining the Confederacy. On August 7, the General Assembly adjourned. Although another session was scheduled for September 17, martial law was declared in Frederick on that day and all pro-Confederate legislators were arrested by federal troops. This ended the special session and quashed the possibility of Maryland remaining neutral in the war.

While these events were occurring in the halls of power, pro-Confederate forces kept the question of Maryland's loyalty in the public eye. The burning of Frederick's courthouse epitomized this pro-Southern movement. Although it is unclear who committed this act, a pro-secession group, the Palmetto Flag Boys, were likely involved. The Flag Boys formed after the pro-Southern rioting in Baltimore and were commanded by Bradley T. Johnson, a prominent secessionist. By the beginning of the war, Johnson's sympathies were well-known and he was in contact with similar organizations throughout Maryland and northern Virginia. On May 8, shortly after the group's formation and following the first special legislative session, Frederick's courthouse burned. Engelbrecht noted the event in his diary: "This Morning between one & two o'clock (a.m.) the Court House in this City was certainly set on fire & burnt nearly out." Later he wrote: "The *Examiner* estimated the loss at $2700 & the County received the money & will build a new Courthouse." While it is unclear who started this fire, Johnson and his twenty-six Flag Boys left for Harpers Ferry the next day. Whether they were guilty or concerned that they would be blamed for the arson is unknown. The Palmetto Flag Boys eventually returned to Frederick with the occupying Confederate army before the Battle of Antietam. Johnson rose through the Confederate military, eventually becoming a brigadier general in the Southern cavalry.

Pro-Union groups were also active in the region. One was the Brengle Home Guards, which also formed in late April 1861. Unlike the Flag Boys, the Home Guards were connected to local authorities. They formed to bolster the Frederick police during the General Assembly's late-April meeting. Engelbrecht described the formation of the group:

> A Company of Home Guards was formed in our city on Wednesday Evening last April 24, 1861 & on the following night the officers were elected. [...] Now over two hundred—they turned out this forenoon & went to the Barracks & were reviewed by Major General Anthony Kimmel, after which the Company received Muskets from the Barracks Armory.

While their purpose was tied to the legislative session, their activities did not end with it. On May 7, the Brengle Home Guards were formally presented their colors from Frederick's female Union supporters. Again, Engelbrecht described the event:

> This afternoon the Ladies (Union Ladies) of this City presented a United States Flag (Stars & Stripes) to the "Brengle Home Guards of Frederick" at the Court House. [...] After the address was delivered the whole assembly sang *The Star Spangled Banner*—the American Band played the national tunes—this was by far the largest meeting ever held at the Court House Square & shows that the people of Frederick County are wide awake and are determined to stick to the Union. Let the consequences be what they may.

This was one of the final events at the courthouse before it burned the following day, an incident that highlighted the divergent paths taken by Frederick residents in the build up to the war.

Frederick was occasionally seized by Confederate forces during their incursions into the north. At other times the city was occupied by large numbers of Union troops. For those citizens with a strong stance on the war, these occupations were frightening interruptions of daily life. Others engaged in commerce with or demonstrated their loyalty to the occupying troops. During early Confederate occupation, Engelbrecht wrote:

> No commotion, or excitement, but all peaceably & quiet. The soldiers are around the town purchasing clothing, shoes, boots, caps & eatables. [...] Many of our citizens left town last night & this morning. The postmaster with all the mail matter and all officers of government appointment, telegraph &c put out. (September 6, 1862)

Although Engelbrecht was not too disturbed by this event, many pro-Union citizens, including governmental officials, left the city.

In the face of periodic occupations, pro-Union citizens continued to support the federal government, as a commemorative event only a couple of months later demonstrates. During the war, George Washington's birthday became a rallying point for Union supporters. Engelbrecht described this holiday in 1862:

> Today Washington's birthday was celebrated by the people of Frederick by the ringing of the bells & the firing of cannon by the military. Two flags were presented by the ladies of Frederick to the First Maryland Regiment under Colonel William P. Maulsby. The presentation was made by James T. Smith & received by William P. Maulsby. Addresses made by both. (The) different Regiments in our neighborhood were present (on) the occasion numbering 4 or 5,000 who paraded through (the) streets. The presentation was made at the veranda of the Junior Hall where nearly all the staff officers were. Major General N. P. Banks, Colonel Geary, General Abercrombie, &c &c were present. After the presentation *The Star Spangled Banner* was sung—led by William D. Reese. And Mrs. General Banks sung in style. Among the singers your humble servant was among the singers and I would remark that I sang the same old *Star Spangled Banner* a few weeks after it was composed say about October 1814. (February 22, 1862)

With the South in revolt, national holidays became important touchstones for Union civilians and soldiers to connect with a broader sense of nationhood.

Later that year the city was occupied by the Army of Northern Virginia during General Robert E. Lee's first northern campaign, which culminated in the Battle of Antietam. With word of the force's movements in early September 1862, Union forces destroyed supplies stored in Frederick to deny them to the Confederate army. Engelbrecht described the events of September 5, 1862:

✧ *Civil War Union troops parade on North Market Street on February 22, 1862, to celebrate George Washington's Birthday.*

> Last night the report is that [Stonewall] Jackson's Army (Rebel Army) were at Benjamin M. Moffat's farm 3 miles below Buckeystown on their way to Frederick. The Provost Marshal received a telegraph despatch [sic], that in the event of the enemy's approaching, to destroy the government stores. Accordingly, about 10 o'clock they commenced burning beds & cots that were stored at "Kemp Hall" corner of Market and Church Street and burnt them in Church Street from the parsonage to the first seminary[...] At the [Frederick Town] Barracks they burnt some stores also at the depot they burnt tents, cots, beds, guns, (muskets). Soldiers clothing & shoes were forgotten which fell into the Rebels hands. In all this commotion, myself & wife heard nothing of it. (September 6, 1862)

Catherine Markell also described this event, noting "Federals burning their stores and 'skedadling' [...] Saw the sick from the Barrack Hospital straggling with bandaged heads etc. towards Pennsylvania. Was greatly excited" (September 5, 1862).

On September 6, 1862, the anticipated Southern army arrived. Engelbrect estimated that ten thousand soldiers were on leave in the city, leading to shortages of products and what he described as "a complete jam." As the army left the city days later, Engelbrecht described the scene, noting:

> They were generally young & hearty men & had been in service so long that they were very much fagged [worn] out. Many were barefooted & some had one shoe & one barefoot. They really looked "ragged & tough". The first 8 or 10 thousand got a tolerable good supply of clothing & shoes & boots but the stores & shops were soon sold out. [...] I was very anxious to see the whole proceedings of an enemy taking a town and living in it. I must say that at no time was I the least alarmed. (Neither was my wife.) We took it coolly & deliberately. [...] One thing I know. We put ourselves into the hands of the Lord who had watched over us so many years & we were fully assured he would not forsake us in time of need. It certainly is a serious thing for an enemy to invade your country & cities. There is generally so much destruction. But I must say the Rebels behaved themselves well, but at the same time the citizen of both parties also treated them well. (September 11, 1862)

✧ *Confederate troops march west on East Patrick Street on September 12, 1862.*

In her own description of these events, Catherine Markell dwelt on the Confederate officers present in town, whom she met as a socially prominent Southern sympathizer. On September 9, she accompanied a group of women to call on the Confederate generals Robert E. Lee, Thomas Jonathan "Stonewall" Jackson, and James Longstreet. Aside from mentioning the difficulty of acquiring food and supplies on September 8, her account romanticizes these figures, overlooking the grim realities of the war, and the practice of slavery that caused it. During the war, Markell collected the signatures of prominent Confederates in an autograph book. She described Lee, who had recently injured his wrists in a riding accident, in her account:

> Both [of Lee's hands] were bandaged almost to the fingertips so that we could but just touch them in shaking the noble old soldier's hand. "Touch them gently, ladies," he said, when we insisted on a handshake. General Pryor called, also General J. E. B. Stuart, the latter is a gay, rollicking cavalier and a great favorite with the girls. (September 9, 1862)

As the Army of Northern Virginia broke camp on September 10, Markell recorded that many Southern supporters, particularly women, displayed their allegiances and interacted with the soldiers. She noted: "Mrs. Douglas displayed a pretty little rebel flag [...] at the window. Fanny Ebert had my southern cross which caused great cheering. I pinned, at his earnest request, a tiny Confederate flag to the hat of a South Carolina soldier as the army passed." One event shocked her on September 7: "General T. J. Jackson attended church at night with Captain [Henry Kyd] Douglass—sat in William Bantz's pew, the second back of ours. Dr. Zacharias prayed for the President of the United States!!" Zacharias' prayer was one example of passive resistance by Frederick's citizens to the Southern forces. However, it may have gone unheard by Jackson. Both Jackson's brother-in-law and Douglass stated that, while devout, Jackson "invariably" fell asleep during church services. While these military occupations were tense exper iences for Frederick's citizens, such subtle resistance occurred. One of them produced a famous piece of Americana.

Whereas Francis Scott Key produced the most iconic verse of the War of 1812, another Frederick resident was the subject of a famous Civil War-era poem. A year after the 1862 Confederate occupation of Frederick, a poem became popular that described the elderly Barbara Fritchie's defiance of Confederate General Stonewall Jackson's order to remove an American flag from her home on West Patrick Street. According to the poem *The Ballad of Barbara Fritchie* by John Greenleaf Whittier, Fritchie stood up to the rest of town, as well as Jackson and his troops, in keeping her American flag hanging. In the poem, she declares "Shoot if you must this old gray head/But spare your country's flag." Impressed by her courage, Jackson replies "Who touches a hair on yon gray head/ Dies like a dog! March on!" While dramatic and evocative, there are many reasons to question the veracity of Whittier's account. There is no hard evidence that the event occurred. No other residents of the town recorded the event at the time, although at least one other Frederick County woman, Mary Quantrell, did resist Confederate forces this way. Engelbrecht, writing on April 8, 1869, and reacting to the popularity of the incident, cast doubt on the event:

> I do not believe one word of it. I live directly opposite [to Fritchie], and for three days I was nearly continually looking at the Rebel army passing the door and nearly the whole army passed our door and should anything like that have occurred I am certain someone of our family would have noticed it.

It is unclear why Fritchie's name was used in this poem, although the poem made Frederick nationally famous for the incident and Barbara Fritchie's descendants capitalized on her sudden fame. They popularized Fritchie's legacy, going so far as to raise money for a patriotic monument to Fritchie in Mount Olivet Cemetery that would rival the Washington Monument in the capital. The monument was much more modest than initially planned, but as a result of this poem, Barbara Fritchie has enjoyed a great deal of fame since the Civil War. A variety of products have been marketed with her name and an automotive derby has been held in her honor. Although her house was torn down in 1869 during an expansion of

Carroll Creek, a smaller-scale recreation of the structure was built and in the twenty-first century remains open to visitors as the Barbara Fritchie House. The poem was also featured in an episode of the classic cartoon *Rockie and Bullwinkle*, in which the hapless moose Bullwinkle acts out the part of Barbara Fritchie as the poem is read.

As the Confederates withdrew, small skirmishes occurred on Patrick Street and

✧ *Barbara Fritchie (1766–1862), c. 1862.*

at the Monocacy Bridge between advancing Union troops and the Southern rearguard on September 12. Markell described the battle on Patrick Street this way:

> About four o'clock a courier informed the generals that the Yankee drums could be heard and the advancing columns of McClellan's army were in sight. Hampton had left and Lee started but the "Cavalier" Stuart waited until his hurried command was obeyed and then formed his men in line of battle immediately in front of our house—where a considerable skirmish occurred. The Confederates slowly retiring toward the mountain—up the Middletown pike. One of the Federal cannon burst at the east end of Patrick Street, killing several men. A piece of our front door railing was shot away. We all retired to the cellar where we found concealed an old Confederate soldier. Mr. Erasmus West, wife, and children and the O'Leary's were here. We all went on the house top after the fight to see McClellan's army enter. Some one hoisted a flag on Robert McPherson's house [...] which a Confederate officer spied and returning almost in face of the enemy, compelled them to take it down.

Engelbrecht also described the events of September 12:

> [T]here was some skirmishing near the Monocacy stone bridge. I distinctly heard 22 cannons fired. This was about 2 o'clock (Friday September 12 1862). Afterwards I went to the roof of Mr. Valentine S. Brunner's warehouse at the depot where I saw (with an opera glass) the Union troops advancing in different squads, & the secession cavalry slowly retreating. The Rebels then came to town through Patrick Street as far as Bentztown just above the bridge. They halted, turned right about & drew their swords & went down street in full speed. They met the advancing Union advance in the Square between Ad_um's House & Groshon's (Carroll Street) where a skirmish took place. No one was killed & several slightly wounded. [...] In about half an hour thereafter the Union Army came flocking into town from nearly every point of the compass south & east. And by seven o'clock the town was full of soldiers nearly all infantry & some cavalry. They then went out Patrick Street to (encamp) headed by Major General A. E. Burnside, but such huzzaing you never did hear.

As Englebrecht's account suggests, while Confederate supporters were visible during the occupation, the Union troops were more popular in Frederick. These skirmishes were a small hint of the confrontation that Lee's invasion of the North precipitated.

The Army of Northern Virginia occupied other Frederick County communities during Lee's 1862 invasion. The occupation of Urbana led to an amusing occurrence during a ball held on September 8 by General J. E. B. Stuart. While resting in Urbana, Stuart invited the ladies of Frederick County to dance with his men at the Landon House to music performed by the Eighteenth Mississippi Cavalry Regimental Band. The house was decorated with Confederate flags and roses and, during the ball, Stuart received word of approaching Northern troops. The men left and confronted a small group of Union cavalry heading toward Frederick. With the threat ended, they returned to the ball, an event remembered alternatively as the Interrupted Ball and the Sabers and Roses Ball.

These forces' maneuvers led to the first major military action of the Civil War in Frederick County: the Battle of South Mountain. This battle—a precursor to the cataclysmic Battle of Antietam—was fought in Crampton's, Turner's, and Fox's gaps: the three main passes across South Mountain. Northern Major General George B. McClellan gained important knowledge of the Army of Northern Virginia's movements following Union troops' discovery of a copy of Lee's Special Order 191 on the Best farm near Monocacy Depot on September 13. With this information, McClellan knew he had to cross South Mountain quickly to catch Lee. Learning of the Union pursuit, Lee sent men into the passes to delay him. McClellan organized his Army of the Potomac into three forces, one for each pass, and sent them against the Army of Northern Virginia's rearguard on September 14. At Crampton's Gap, the southernmost pass, the Union Fourth Corps greatly outnumbered the Confederate defenders, but delayed their advance for three hours after coming under fire in Burkittsville. Once on the move, Union forces quickly overran the Confederate positions as they pressed steadily up the mountain. Due to the delays, the federal troops crossed the mountain too late to relieve Harpers Ferry, then under siege by Jackson. At Turner's and Fox's gaps, the Union First and Ninth Corps seized the high points of the passes after an all-day battle. Lee recognized that the Southern position could not hold much longer and withdrew his forces after dark.

✧ *The Gathland Civil War Correspondents Memorial Arch erected in Crampton's Gap on South Mountain near Burkittsville.*

By this point, almost five thousand men were dead, wounded, or missing.

While the Battle of South Mountain marked an important Union victory at this stage in the war, Lee succeeded in reorganizing his scattered command along the Sharpsburg Ridge. The armies clashed again west of Frederick County around Antietam Creek. Fought on September 17, the Battle of Antietam marked not only the end of Lee's 1862 foray into the North, but also the bloodiest day in American history, with over twenty-three thousand men killed, wounded, or missing.

The residents of neighboring Frederick County faced the aftermath of this struggle in Washington County. To deal with the almost unimaginable human cost of the battle, the inhabitants of Frederick used their public and private buildings as impromptu military hospitals. Many citizens provided their buildings to care for the wounded soldiers, at times without seeking recompense for room and board or for expenses incurred in cleaning and repairing the structures. The scale of the injured is difficult to fathom. Roughly ten thousand wounded or ill soldiers were treated in Frederick over the course of the war. Most of these were casualties of the Battle of Antietam. Recalling the event, Lavinia Hooper, who was nine years old in 1862, described the wounded:

> There were lots of wounded brought into Frederick almost every day. And it was up to us to see that they got something decent to eat. My mother baked pies and we would take the pies up on straw baskets to the Hessian Barricks [sic] and the Lutheran Church which was filled with the wounded from both sides. We'd walk in and hand the food directly to the soldiers. Sometimes they would talk to us and sometimes they were too sick to talk. Lots of times I can recall standing on Market Street, which was a dirt road then and how we used to watch the wagons bringing the wounded into Frederick for us to look after. There was so much blood dripping out of the back of the wagons and falling on the dirt road that eventually the mud became red as the wagon wheels ploughed through the streets.

Dr. George Diehl, the Evangelical Lutheran Church's pastor, also described the event:

> Instead of the preacher's familiar voice, the anthems of the choir, or the response of the congregation, we heard the groans and painful exclamations of the prostrate youthful soldiers. The congregation and flourishing Sunday School were scattered. The really clear and beautifully toned bells were hushed.

Many churches were used as hospitals, as they were large, public structures with congregations willing to provide assistance to the wounded, the sick, and the dying. The Lutheran Church was one such church. Although it took soldiers from both sides of the conflict, the hospital was staffed by pro-Confederate women. Henry Tisdale, a grocery store clerk from Massachusetts who had enlisted in the Thirty-Fifth Massachusetts Infantry, noted this aspect of the hospital. After being wounded in Fox's Gap, he was treated in Middletown and then in Frederick's Lutheran Church. He described the church in his diary:

> A rough board floor was laid over the tops of the pews. Folding iron bedsteads with mattresses, clean white sheets, pillows, blankets, and clean underclothing, hospital dressing gowns, slippers, etc. were furnished us freely. The citizens came in twice a day with a host of luxuries, cordials, etc. for our comfort. The church finely finished off within, well ventilated and our situation as pleasant and comfortable as could be made. A few rebel wounded were in the building. Some of the citizens showed them special attention bringing them articles of food, etc. and giving none to the others. The surgeons put a stop to this however by telling them that they must distribute to all alike or they would not be allowed to visit the hospital at all, this was much to our satisfaction.

Along with churches, schools opened their doors for patients. Because a state-sponsored lottery had funded its construction, the Frederick Female Seminary, located in what is now Winchester Hall, was considered a public building. This, combined with its size, made it a clear candidate for use as a hospital following Antietam. Soldiers were housed in the west wing, while classes continued in its east wing. To return to its original mission, Hiram Winchester asked the army to move the patients in December 1862. However, crowded conditions at another hospital caused an outbreak of gangrene, and the school's kitchens fed patients in the Lutheran and Methodist Episcopal churches, so Frederick's medical director John J. Milhau refused, at least until the church hospitals could be closed. The churches were cleared the following month and the female seminary hospital closed in January 1863. After the closure, Winchester noted that the buildings were in "a most wretched filthy and dilapidated condition." He eventually received almost three hundred dollars for these damages, but this did not consider the loss of tuition. Winchester had continuing problems convincing people to send their daughters there, as an 1864 letter to the Quartermaster's Office shows. In the letter, he writes that "my old friends still tell me they do not like to send their daughters here to sleep in the same rooms that were used for a hospital." He assuaged public concerns about this in the Winchester *Examiner* on August 12, 1865, which advertised the seminary's reopening on September 1, 1865. Visitation Academy was also used as a hospital, even though sixty Southern boarding students who were unable to return home due to the war still resided there. Other students left, while those who remained were sequestered from the soldiers, their daily educational routines being adhered to as much as possible.

Hotels also became hospitals. The three-story United States Hotel, located near the B&O Railroad Station on Market Street, had fifty rooms for customers. This central site near a major transportation hub was invaluable in housing wounded soldiers. The need was so desperate that the hotel's owner, Norman B. Harding, was only given fifteen minutes notice to vacate the building with his wife. The hotel served as a hospital until January 23, 1863, and was quick to reopen in February after a thorough cleaning and repair. While it was a hospital, the Hardings provided food and other supplies to the wounded residents.

Other wounded soldiers were housed at another prominent Frederick landmark: the Frederick Town Barracks. With a new war, the barracks was already in use for military purposes. The previous year, it was the site of U.S. General Hospital No. 1 from August 8–26, 1861. The barracks, along with nearby Coppersmith Hall and Albaugh House, was the site of a military depot, hospital, and barracks for Union troops. The hospital temporarily moved to Baltimore until late 1861, but passing forces continued to use the barracks as a camp and storage depot throughout the war. Following the battles of South Mountain and Antietam, it was again a hospital, housing Union and Confederate wounded.

Along with temporarily housing wounded soldiers, other Frederick structures were used as storehouses for military supplies such as uniforms and food. While less disruptive to the city's functioning when compared to the flood of wounded and dying soldiers, this usage created a long-term impact for residents. Private residences were also sometimes selected for government or military use. For example, John J. Wilson's house, built in 1849 just west of the German Reformed Church, was used by the Union as a provost office, jail, and guard house by December 1861. The following September, it was officially rented to serve as the provost marshal's guard house. It was also used as an overflow hospital site after hospitals in Winchester, Virginia, closed in July 1862. In 1864, Wilson, the homeowner, submitted a claim to the government for damages, stating that the house had been almost new at the beginning of the war, but that it had been damaged by the prisoners held there. He could not get his insurance policy reinstated and, in 1868, an insurance inspector described the property as follows:

> I have never seen a building in such a dilapidated condition. Nearly all the casing and woodwork has been destroyed with the exception of the third floor and the joists and framing of the roof. Every outside opening, windows and doors, have been destroyed and the building as much exposed as it possibly can be.

The German Reformed Church purchased the house and lot in 1870, planning to use it as an orphanage. However, this never occurred and the house was demolished by 1887.

Every Frederick County resident was affected by the war, and those on the home-front confronted it in many ways. Troops moved throughout the region and soldiers disrupted everyday routines. Both sides confiscated property for the war effort, which included food, animals, and medical supplies. Occupying armies restricted travel and required citizens to have passes to enter and leave towns. The diminished potential of farms and industrial centers led to product shortages and worsened an existing economic depression. Frederick served as a base of operations by both Northern and Southern armies for many reasons. Besides being in a county geographically linked to both Union and Confederate states, it was also a transportation hub, with the B&O Railroad, the National Road, and major roads to Baltimore and Washington, D.C. Frederick was also a relatively modern city, with paved roads, water service, and gas lighting. These factors helped make Frederick a thriving city, but also brought the war home to county residents.

✧ *The B&O Railroad Station, constructed in 1854, was integral to Frederick's hospitals during the Civil War and to the city's growing industry following the war. In this November 1911 photograph, the station is decorated for a visit by President Taft.*

While the wounded were still being cared for in Frederick after Antietam, Abraham Lincoln passed through the city on October 4 after visiting General McClellan's Army of the Potomac, which was encamped around Sharpsburg in the battle's aftermath. He visited Brigadier General George Hartsuff, who was recovering at lodgings on Record Street from a wound suffered in the East Woods during

Antietam. Outside the building, he gave a short speech to the assembled crowd:

> In my present position, it is hardly proper for me to make speeches. Every word is so closely noted that it will not do to make trivial ones, and I cannot be expected to be prepared to make a matured one just now. If I were as I have been most of my life, I might perhaps, talk amusing to you for half an hour, and it wouldn't hurt anybody; but as it is, I can only return my sincere thanks for the compliment paid our cause and our common country.

Lincoln made a similar speech at Frederick's downtown B&O Railroad depot before travelling back to Washington, D.C. By January 7, 1863, most of the recovering soldiers had been transferred to General Hospital No. 1, although according to the *Frederick Examiner* a primary school on North Market Street still contained patients. By November, the *Examiner* reported that over three hundred soldiers remained at General Hospital No. 1.

Frederick again hosted large numbers of soldiers in the summer of 1863, as General Lee refocused his attention on the region, which culminated in the battle of Gettysburg. With Confederate forces in the area, many of Frederick's prominent Unionists and federal personnel fled the city. Rather than destroy the supplies held in the city, Union soldiers distributed many of these resources to citizens, including three thousand fifty-pound boxes of hardtack. Engelbrecht recorded that "The town I suppose will be filled with crackers for some time." The Confederate First Maryland Cavalry entered Frederick on June 20, 1863, briefly skirmishing with Major Henry A. Cole's Union cavalry. This occupation was short-lived, as the Southerners were driven out the next day by twenty-five members of Cole's Cavalry, who fought a small skirmish on Patrick Street. Engelbrecht noted that, "They came near enough to fire at the hindmost and shot at least 20 or 30 rounds. [...] I happened to be at the bend just as they came by in full speed firing as fast as they could." Markell also described the events, noting "Attended church and Sunday School. Soldiers skirmishing in street in front of our house. School dismissed in haste here, we could [not?] get into Patrick Street for the skirmishing."

While Confederate forces did not pass through Frederick en masse during this campaign, many Union troops did, and they were greeted by many of the residents. On June 30, Union troops even maneuvered a pontoon bridge up Market Street, taking two to three hours in the process. The bridge was used on the Susquehannah River. Colonel P. Regis de Trobriand of the Union Third Corps, later described his journey through Frederick this way:

> All the houses were draped; all the women were at the windows, waving their handkerchiefs; all the men were at their doors waving their hats. In the middle of the principal street a pretty child, ten or twelve years of age, had left a group collected on the sill of a house of modest appearance. Her mother had just given her a large bouquet, pointing me out with her hand. The little girl came bravely forward in front of the horses, holding towards me her little arms full of flowers. I leaned from my saddle to receive the fragrant present, and she said, with a rosy smile, "Good luck to you, General!" I thanked her to the best of my ability. I would have liked to have embraced the little messenger with her happy wishes, but the march could not halt for so small an affair. When she rejoined her family, running along, I turned to kiss my hand to her in adieu. She nodded her head, and, blushing, hid it in her mother's bosom. "Well!" said I, riding on, "that little girl ought to bring me good fortune."

Trobriand and his men went on to fight in the infamous Wheatfield at Gettysburg on July 2. Despite heavy casualties, they held out against Confederate Major General John Bell Hood's division before being reinforced. Not only did Trobriand survive the battle, he was not injured, possibly causing him to recall his encounter with the little girl in Frederick.

During the troops' passage before and after Gettysburg, the United States Hotel was used as a Union headquarters. Major General Joseph Hooker used it in late June 1863, prior to his partially accidental resignation as commander of the Army of the Potomac on June 27 after arguing with his superior, Major General Henry Halleck, about holding Harpers Ferry. Hooker's replacement, George Meade, who received his command while camped outside Frederick at Prospect Hall on June 28, stayed at the hotel following Gettysburg. He used it as a headquarters until Lee's escape across the Potomac on July 14, 1863. With Meade based there, Frederick was again filled with Northern soldiers and Southern prisoners of war. Markell wrote on June 28 that: "Could not go out on account of the jam in the streets. Soldiers everywhere." Engelbrecht echoed her sentiments, noting on July 6 that "The whole town is in commotion. Nothing but soldiers & soldiers. Posterity could hardly conceive what a vast number of soldiers have passed our town. Within the last year, both armies together, I think three hundred thousand is within bounds." On July 8, he recorded that "The truth is that [the soldiers] all passing all day and nearly all night. Such an incessant racket that you can hardly carry on a conversation in the shop."

In the Civil War, the line between civilians and soldiers was not always completely clear. This was seen in Frederick County through the activities of spies for both sides. These individuals passed information on troop movements to the other side and, although not uniformed soldiers, placed their lives in extreme risk. For the Union, much of this information eventually passed through the Bureau of Military Information when it was organized in 1863 under Hooker. The bureau's third-in-command in June 1863, John Babcock, used Frederick as a base. During the Antietam campaign, he had worked with Allen Pinkerton, who operated an intelligence network as a private contractor for the Union. In Frederick,

Babcock was suspected by many Confederate sympathizers when the Confederate First Maryland Cavalry passed through on June 20, 1863. These suspicions were raised due to his association with known spy James Greenwood, a citizen of Martinsburg, Virginia. Fearing discovery and execution by the Confederate cavalry, Babcock prepared to flee Frederick with his official papers. He found pickets guarding the major routes into and out of the city. As the cavalry entered Frederick, Babcock was in front of the Central House Hotel, which he labeled "a notorious rebel hole." With the presence of these forces, Babcock was in immediate danger. Although forced to destroy his papers, he lost his pursuers in a large crowd and escaped to "a private house in a remote part of the town." When the Confederates withdrew to the edge of town the next day, Babcock ran the pickets on the B&O Railroad with a handcar and fled to Baltimore. There he telegraphed his superior, Colonel George Henry Sharpe. On June 24, Babcock provided invaluable intelligence to the Union military about the Army of Northern Virginia's movements. As the first credible source to report these movements, he alerted federal forces that the Confederates had crossed the Potomac River at Shepherdstown, but had not advanced on Frederick and the passes at South Mountain. This indicated that General Lee was marching north rather than east, a move that ended in the Battle of Gettysburg.

Confederate spies were also active in the region throughout the war. One, a man named Richardson, was captured by Major General John Buford's cavalry near Woodsboro after Gettysburg. Richardson's capture made the *New York Times* on July 12, 1863, which reported that he raised suspicion by possessing drawings of Baltimore's defenses and a letter for Confederate Lieutenant General Richard S. Ewell that spoke for his reliability and his ability to provide information. He was found guilty at a quick military hearing on July 5 and was hung on a tree near Frederick. He remained on the tree for several days as citizens took pieces of his clothing and the tree's bark as souvenirs. One federal soldier, Captain Stephen Minot Weld described the scene: "About a mile out from town I passed the body of a rebel spy, hung by Buford, naked and discolored, still dangling to a tree—a fearful warning to such rascals. He had been accustomed to sell papers and maps in our army."

✧ *General George Meade became the commander of the Army of the Potomac at Prospect Hall on June 27, 1863. Prospect Hall, pictured here, was later used as a Union headquarters during a battle in West Frederick prior to the Battle of Monocacy in 1864.*

Confederate forces occupied Frederick County once more, in the summer of 1864. Union victories the previous year, notably at Gettysburg and Vicksburg, had the Confederacy on the defensive. As a result, Lieutenant General Ulysses Grant had the bulk of the Union army engaged in a broad offensive across Virginia, including at Richmond and in the Shenandoah Valley, which was an important source of food for the Confederacy. With Grant pulling troops out of numerous northern forts to replace his casualties, this left few men to defend Washington, D.C., and other important facilities in the region. General Lee was pressured to exploit this weakness and defend the Shenandoah Valley. Although reluctant to recommit troops from the defense of Richmond, Lee sent Lieutenant General Jubal Early to attack the North. The ideal conclusion of this campaign was to threaten the Union capitol and to free Southern prisoners of war held at Point Lookout, Maryland. Early forced Union Major General David Hunter's troops to retreat from Lynchburg, Virginia, on June 18, opening a relatively clear route north. He moved along the Shenandoah Valley toward the Potomac River without encountering Northern forces until arriving in Jefferson County, West Virginia. This was now part of a northern state after western Virginia had achieved statehood in 1863. Early fought numerous engagements there, including one in Harpers Ferry, before entering Maryland. While moving through Maryland, Early demanded payments from numerous towns, threatening to burn the towns if these demands were not met. One ransomed community was Middletown, where, on July 7, the Confederate Second Maryland Cavalry under Major Harry Gilmor demanded meat and bread from each family, which was provided. The next day, more Confederates, under Major General Robert Ransom and Brigadier General Bradley Johnson, demanded more rations, which were provided again. This virtually depleted Middletown of its meat, sugar, and coffee. That Confederate forces demanded food and supplies illustrates the South's difficult position due to federal control of the Shenandoah Valley and its agricultural resources. That evening, Early

✧ *The City Hotel in Frederick in the early twentieth century.*

demanded that Middletown pay a $5,000 ransom, an amount that the town burgess, William J. Irving, challenged as unreasonable. Early refused to relent and demanded that $1,500 be paid the next morning, with the rest provided that evening. After collecting the first payment in the morning, Early's men moved on, with a portion of his infantry left to collect the balance. Luckily for the citizens of Middletown, the Confederate infantry fled from Union cavalry and left without the money. Early also ransomed Hagerstown and Chambersburg.

Early attempted to ransom Frederick on July 9 after arriving in the city that morning. The Confederates demanded thousands of pounds of food while at the home of Doctor Richard T. Hammond, a Confederate sympathizer, who lived on the northwest corner of Market and Second Streets. As during previous occupations, most of the federal supplies and Union wounded had been removed before the Confederates arrived, which Early learned of while waiting at Hammond's home. Frustrated by this news, he issued a demand to Mayor William G. Cole at city hall that the city pay two-hundred thousand dollars. Early was then alerted by the sounds of battle at Monocacy Junction. Accounts differ on how quickly he left for the battle, but his staff remained for the ransom. As at Middletown, town officials responded with incredulity at the scope of the Confederate demands for cash. They pointed out that the city only had an annual tax revenue of eight thousand dollars. However, Early's staff saw the wealth displayed by Frederick's banks, large homes, and prosperous businesses and responded that they felt the amount could be provided within the time frame. As the battle raged south of the city, local officials and prominent citizens bought time, hoping that the Union forces would prevail against Early's larger force. As the battle turned against the federal troops that afternoon, Cole agreed to the demands. A coalition of five major city banks—the Fredericktown Savings Institution, the Central Bank, the Frederick County Bank, the Franklin Savings Bank, and the Farmers and Mechanics Bank—provided the capital in a set of wicker baskets to Lieutenant Colonel William M. Allen, Early's chief of ordnance. Allen gave his word not to take additional resources, such as food or equipment, without payment. Major J. R. Braithwaite, Early's bonded quartermaster, provided a written receipt for the money to Cole. Local legend suggests that the staff celebrated this payment over dinner at a Frederick restaurant, where they partook of champagne and ice cream. Regardless of their culinary decisions, the officers took the money to Early. They left behind a detachment of soldiers to guard against angry citizens. While there, these soldiers entered the Bantz warehouse on Brewery's Alley, retrieving new military blankets and leaving their old, worn blankets in the street.

Although the city's banks saved Frederick, they still expected to be repaid. After four years of negotiations, the city and the banks came up with a payment plan involving one hundred thousand dollars in interest-bearing bonds with a six percent interest rate and a thirty-year term. After refinancing several times, the final payment was made on September 29, 1951. To commemorate the events, the twenty thousand dollar payment was placed in one of the wicker baskets used for the original payment. In 1889, the city also began to petition the U.S. Congress to help repay the banks, given that if the ransom had not been paid, well over two hundred thousand dollars worth of military supplies stored throughout Frederick would have been lost. However, a letter written by resident Thomas Gorsuch shortly after the battle suggest that plenty of valuables were lost during the occupation, noting that "The town escaped any serious damage by paying $200,000 ransom money; the community surrounding is pretty well striped [sic] of every thing, stock, money, clothing and every thing [the Confederates] could use or get away."

As local communities struggled with Early's ransom demands, Union forces responded to the invasion. While Early pushed for Washington and Point Lookout, additional Union troops were sent by Major General Lew Wallace on July 3 to reinforce those at Monocacy Junction, a critical position along the B&O Railroad where the railroad was close to the National Road, the Georgetown Pike, and the Monocacy River. News reached Wallace about the fighting at Harpers Ferry, but he kept his forces at the junction, where the terrain favored the defenders due to the difficulty of moving wagons and artillery across the river. The thirteen hundred troops deployed at Monocacy Junction included many so-called Hundred Days Men—volunteers who served one hundred day terms to take over routine duties for veteran troops—with relatively few experienced troops. Wallace spread his troops along six miles of the river to protect the bridges and fords in an attempt to delay the Confederate advance and give Union reinforcements time to reach the nation's capitol. Numerous skirmishes and military operations occurred in the region around Frederick before the battle. General Bradley T. Johnson, the organizer of Frederick's Palmetto Flag Boys and now a Confederate cavalry officer, led his soldiers against a mixed force of Northern infantry, cavalry, and artillery in the farms west of Frederick on July 7 and 8. At the same time, Confederate Brigadier General John McCausland's cavalry brigade arrived and severed the telegraph line connecting Maryland Heights with Washington, D.C., and Baltimore before marching on Monocacy Junction.

Reinforced by five thousand men under Union Brigadier General James B. Ricketts, Wallace's forces occupied the higher ground on the east side of the river, as well as some quickly prepared fortifications and existing structures. Initial fighting on July 9 made Early overestimate the size of the Union forces and adopt a more cautious approach. After a failed attempt to outflank Wallace's men with cavalry, the Confederates launched a three-part attack on the Northern line, which overwhelmed the left flank of the Union army and eventually forced Wallace to withdraw his forces toward Baltimore. Between the two armies, over two thousand men were killed, wounded, or captured during this engagement. Although the Union lost the battle, the largely untested Northern soldiers had succeeded in their broader goal: to delay the Confederate advance on Washington, D.C., and to give reinforcements time to arrive by ship from Virginia. By July 11, Early arrived within the District of Columbia and could see the U.S. Capitol Building through his field glasses, but his men were too tired following the events at Monocacy and the long, hot march to Washington to press an attack on Fort Stevens, one of the outlying Union defensive positions. As Early's forces approached the capitol, Union ships docked in the harbor. The fresh troops contained in these vessels narrowly arrived in time to reinforce the city's defenses and halted the Confederates. With these men in place, Early withdrew and crossed back into Virginia on July 13. Although Wallace lost the Battle of Monocacy, he and his men succeeded in their broader objective and prevented Early's attack on Washington, D.C.

POST CIVIL WAR LIFE

The Battle of Monocacy was the last major engagement in Frederick County during the Civil War. With the end of the war in 1865 the nation changed in many ways, most significantly with universal emancipation. However, thousands were dead and virtually no family was untouched by the war, particularly in a border state such as Maryland. The war not only fundamentally reshaped the South's economy and culture, but changed the nation as a whole. It spurred industrialization and birthed new technologies, including the preservation and refrigeration techniques that were critical to returning the war's dead home for burial. These technologies revolutionized methods of preserving and transporting food after the war, industrializing many aspects of agriculture and expanding the reach of large farms. With so much death, burial practices shifted. Holidays to memorialize the war's dead became nationally important, with separate days for North and South. Engelbrecht described early celebrations of each of these holidays. Here is his description of an early Northern Decoration Day:

> This afternoon at 3 o'clock (Monday May 30, 1870) the graves of the Union soldiers, who were killed in battle or died of wounds &c were decorated in Mount Olivet Cemetery & the church grave yards in Frederick. Captain William Glessner was the commander assisted by Captain Walter Saunders and ladies. Prayer by the Reverend Robert H. Williams and an address by Doctor Lewis E. Steiner. Singing at the graves and at the conclusion *Shall we know each other there* was sung by a special choir.

His description on June 4, 1870, of the Southern equivalent was more sparse: "The Rebels had a decoration this afternoon at Mount Olivet Cemetery where 500 Rebel dead are buried. They were principally such as were wounded at the battle of Antietam, Gettysburg, Monocacy &c." Solemn commemorations of sacrifice were not the only holidays celebrated for the events of the war. For both newly freed slaves and Maryland's free black population, emancipation became a major holiday and was annually celebrated in Frederick County until 1939. From at least 1865 through the remainder of the nineteenth century, emancipation was celebrated with picnics in nearby woods until 1903, when the holiday was observed at the county fairgrounds. The event was often observed with a parade, in which African-American social clubs and societies marched with community children, all done up in their Sunday best. Engelbrecht noted that the first parade on August 23, 1865, was two squares long. Patriotic displays were a common element. Engelbrect described the event on September 2, 1868, which was held in Worman's woods, as follows: "They turned out in style with the American flag flying. 'The Union forever, Hurrah boys, Hurrah.'" The next year, emancipation was celebrated

✧ *Built four years after the battle, the Gambrill House speaks to the influence of James Gambrill, the owner of the Gambrill, or Araby, Mill, which witnessed the fighting and served as a Union field hospital during the fighting.*

✧ *The old Araby Church at Monocacy Battlefield, c. 1920. The 14th New Jersey Monument is visible in the background.*

over two days and Engelbrecht provided a lengthy and powerful description of the event on August 19, 1869:

> John M. Langston Esquire (colored), a lawyer from Oberlin, Ohio addressed the first day meeting. There was a great turnout among the colored friends, and great rejoicing. And well may they rejoice "we hold these truths to be self evident, that all men are created equal, and are endowed by their creator with certain inalienable rights among which are Life, liberty & the pursuit of happiness." Thank God for so much of the Declaration of Independence. Let these anniversaries be continued to the latest posterity.

Many challenges remained for this now universally emancipated population, but these picnics suggest the strong community ties that had developed even through slavery; ties which could now be publically demonstrated.

Although the Emancipation Proclamation ended slavery following Antietam in states in open rebellion, slaves in the rest of the nation remained in bondage until the passage of the Thirteenth Amendment in 1865. Once they were free, the struggle for equal rights was far from over, particularly given the scientific, religious, and cultural justifications for slavery. These theories questioned the equal capabilities of people descended from African populations, and most white Americans believed them even after the war. Variations of these theories continue to be used to justify racial inequality in the twenty-first century. Before the war, in 1860, out of the eight thousand residents of Frederick listed in the census, six hundred were free blacks. Many had industrial occupations and generally lived on the northern and southern edges of the city near their places of employment. With emancipation, many ex-slaves moved into Kleinhart's Alley and, beginning in the 1870s and 1880s, a large African-American neighborhood formed on South Bentz and West All Saints Streets, which remains a major African-American center in Frederick in the twenty-first century. This neighborhood developed its own religious and social organizations, as well as businesses that largely catered to community members who were uncomfortable patronizing white-owned businesses. Much of this discomfort likely came from policies that prevented African-Americans from trying on or returning clothing and eating in restaurants. Many businesses opened in African-American neighborhoods were operated out of the owner's home. Similar, predominantly black communities, such as Sunnyside, were scattered throughout Frederick County.

Religious institutions faced these challenges as well. Some churches were originally integrated, but over time many white parishioners moved to new structures, leaving the old buildings to their African-American counterparts. One example was First Missionary Baptist Church on West All Saints Street. Built before the revolution in 1773, the church was home to a white congregation. With the neighborhood's changing demographics during the Civil War, the church was given to black residents in 1863, eventually becoming First Missionary Baptist Church in 1875. In the early twenty-first century, the congregation remains active in Frederick in a new location on Swallowtail Drive. Another church historically located on West All Saints Street shares a similar history. The Asbury United Methodist Church was descended from the Old Hill Church on East All Saints Street. As with First Missionary, the church's white congregation transferred the structure to the African-American community in 1864. Asbury United Methodist joined the General Assembly of Maryland in 1868 and, with this official incorporation, became Asbury United Methodist Episcopal Church. Its present building was dedicated in 1921 and the church remains a fixture of Frederick. Throughout its history, it has been an important social and spiritual hub of the African-American community. Numerous social clubs have formed within its congregation and its basement has been used as an entertainment venue and housed a basketball league. More recently, it partnered with Trinity United Methodist Church to hold joint seminars on race relations. Other historically black churches exist throughout the county, including Quinn Chapel African Methodist Episcopal Church in Frederick.

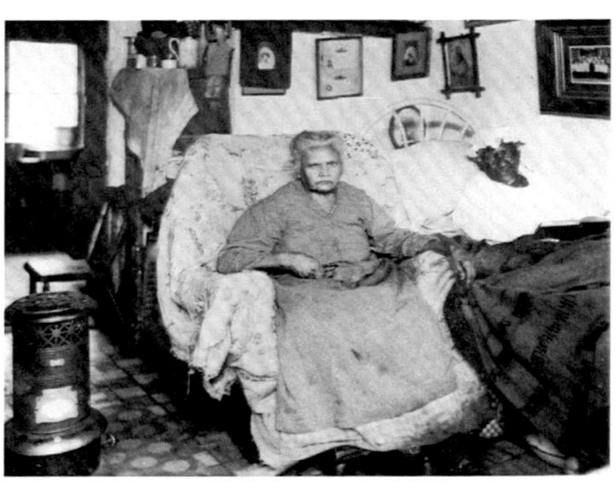

✧ *Anna Mary Sprow, who was enslaved in Frederick County, with her daughter Ruauua Davis in Sprow's home on Kleinhart's Alley, c. 1935.*

Segregation before and after the Civil War not only separated Frederick's white and black citizens in life, but also often in death. An entry in Jacob Engelbrecht's diary from November 24, 1824, suggests this state of affairs:

> Died last night in the 85 year of his age (Negro) Adam Coors. He will be buried on the Lutheran graveyard this day at 3 o'clock with all the rites & privileges of a Lutheran. He was the only black man that was a regular (confirmed) member of the Lutheran Church in this town, which church he assisted in building, in 1754 or 55. He was formerly a slave to Mr. Michael Roemer, one of the founders of the church. He was the most regular church-man that belong to "our Parish" and although he is the first black man that is buried on the Lutheran graveyard I believe there is not one individual objection to his being interred thereon. For my own part, he has my hearty assent.

One African-American cemetery was established before the Civil War by the Beneficial Society of the Laboring Sons of Frederick in 1851. Social clubs and fraternal organizations such as the Laboring Sons were common throughout the nineteenth century within both the white and black communities. Ensuring the burial of members was an important aspect of these organizations, along with assisting their deceased fraternal brothers' widows and orphans. The Laboring Sons cemetery was placed on Chapel Alley between Fifth and Sixth streets. Over time, faced with dwindling membership in the society, the cemetery fell into disrepair and, at the request of the remaining members, the city took over the property in 1949. Although the city pledged to establish a memorial park on the grounds for the fifteen hundred people buried there, the city quickly reversed this agreement and, in 1950, began buying playground equipment for a park on the site. City officials had workers remove the tombstones, but left the bodies interred. Even though hundreds of tombstones were

✧ *A hunting party of several men with their hounds pose for a picture, c. 1880.*

✧ *With its proximity to Washington, D.C., Frederick's citizens often witnessed national events directly. At this Republican political rally in 1888, the campaign of Benjamin Harrison rolled a large ball through the streets. The ball was made in the west and was pulled from state to state by hand to promote Harrison's campaign.*

removed, workers only recorded 160 names from them. Although period newspapers note that several skeletons were disturbed during the park's construction, in 1999, researchers found that hundreds remained buried in unmarked graves in the park. In memory of those buried there, the playground equipment was removed in 2000 and in 2003 the park was converted into a meditative space. Many other historically African-American cemeteries remain throughout the county, such as Fairview Cemetery in Frederick.

As Frederick County's demographic and social makeup changed in the latter half of the nineteenth century, so too did its economic output. With the Civil War's end, the county's farms suffered due to the movements of troops through the region during the war, which destroyed houses, barns, and fields. As a result of this damage and increasing competition from Midwestern corn and wheat producers, the region's farmers suffered economically throughout the 1870s. As a result, many regional farmers shifted from raising wheat to producing dairy products. These products were increasingly valuable because farmers' ability to get milk to market before it spoiled improved thanks to increasing access to preservation technologies, such as refrigerated rail cars.

The fortunes of craftspeople also changed following the Civil War. From 1860 until 1880, there was a downturn in the production of handmade pottery in the county for many reasons, including economic damage from the war, increasing urbanization, and growing production of manufactured pottery and canned goods. Finer pottery and stoneware from other parts of the county and from England were increasingly accessible to consumers, who were becoming concerned about the lead used to make earthenware. While pottery manufacturing decreased, furniture production increased. During the 1880s, artisanal furniture workshops became increasingly mechanized. In Frederick, this furniture production was centered on East Patrick Street and South Market Street, including businesses such as C. C. Carty's, C. E. Cline's, and Obenderfer and Son.

Following the Civil War, Frederick County continued to industrialize, a process begun earlier in the century with the region's mills and iron furnaces.

✧ *Many businesses thrived in Frederick after the Civil War. Many met the everyday needs of the town's residents, such as this 1895 image of Sahm & Dill Hardware and Cutlery, which was located on the corner of Market and Second Streets.*

✧ *D&G Mill manufactured agricultural feed in the twentieth century in Frederick near Carroll Creek, which was the heart of the city's industrial enterprises.*

✧ *Point of Rocks flooded by the Potomac River in 1889, in which much of the town, including the railroad tracks, was under water.*

Although this period saw a decline in iron production, the county's vibrant milling industry continued to expand as new technologies streamlined the process. By the 1870s, overshot mill wheels were being replaced by turbines and steam engines, which prevented mills from being tied so closely to water sources. As a result, many successful millers moved closer to cities for greater access to modes of transportation and cheaper labor. A milling industry began to develop in Frederick. Kemp's Steam Flouring Mills was constructed on Caroll Street in 1872 near the B&O branch depot for greater access to the railroad. In 1878, James Gambrill, who owned the Araby Mills south of Frederick, expanded and bought a steam-powered mill on South Caroll Street. Here, they produced popular brands, such as "Best Araby" and "Unsurpassed." The stone building was destroyed by fire in 1893, but it was rebuilt by 1897 and the business was rebranded as the Frederick City Milling Company.

New technologies not only facilitated existing industries, but also led to the development of new ones. Canning emerged in the last half of the nineteenth century in Frederick County. With rich farmland and major transportation routes, Frederick County was in an ideal position to produce canned goods for the burgeoning U.S. population. The first cannery established in Frederick County was built on West All Saints Street in Frederick in 1869 by Louis McMurray. He invented an automated machine to seal the cans, which increased production by over two hundred percent and allowed for the use of unskilled labor in the process. McMurray's business expanded quickly and by 1873 his factory was canning up to fifteen hundred acres of product a year. His operation was nationally known and he received recognition at major international expositions, including awards for canned sugar corn at the 1876 Philadelphia Centennial Exposition and for canned oysters at the 1878 Paris Exposition. Instead of relying solely on regional farmers, McMurray supplemented his canning operations with produce from his own 2,400 acre farm in southern Frederick County. By 1886, he employed over one thousand men, women, and children on a seasonal basis and his was the largest corn-canning factory in the United States. With this vast workforce, one contemporary wrote that canning "alone supported the working classes of Frederick in a large measure for years." During the last half of the nineteenth century, freed slaves found employment in the cannery. However, problems also came with this expansion. In 1886 this

✧ *Fire company United No. 3's horse-drawn fire truck.*

✧ *Frederick's industrial district along Carroll Creek was prone to flooding through much of the city's history prior to flood control efforts in the late 1970s. This image shows the flood damage on West Patrick Street during an 1868 flood.*

✧ *The Gorsuch family of Catoctin Furnace.*

vast industrial operation came to the attention of the Frederick County Health Department, which charged the plant with numerous sanitary problems. These charges included improper disposal of waste byproducts such as cornhusks and horse manure, contamination of local water supplies by wastewater discharges, rotten vegetables in the factory, and unsanitary privies for workers. This last issue was particularly dangerous and the department blamed the cannery for a diphtheria outbreak in Frederick.

Even with these issues the canning industry grew during the 1890s. McMurray expanded, building a second cannery near New Market to replace the Frederick buildings, which were then torn down. Other canneries emerged during this period, including the Frederick City Packing Company, the Buckeystown Packing Company, and Hewitt's Tomato Canning Factory in Frederick. One major cannery, the Monocacy Valley Canning Company of Frederick, opened in 1898 and sold their goods across the country, producing over six million cans a year while employing as many as five hundred workers. By 1832 there were ten canning plants in the county, including locations in Frederick, Adamstown, Monrovia, Thurmont, and Woodsboro.

As the nineteenth century continued, Frederick County's woolen industry slowed down. By 1870 the county's eight woolen mills only employed thirty-eight people. By the turn of the twentieth century, only one of these woolen mills remained. While this period saw a downturn in wool production, another industry replaced it: the production of ready-made clothing. This new type of clothing was widely accepted by American consumers by the 1890s. By the 1880s, there were fourteen knitting mills in Frederick County, including the Union Manufacturing Company, which was founded in 1887 as the Frederick Seamless Hosiery Company to make half-hose for men. The factory employed fifteen women, the result of a conscious decision by management to make opportunities for female workers. Its factory in eastern Frederick included a dye house and a printing plant and produced hosiery and shirts. Many of these clothing manufacturers continued the Catoctin Furnace's industrial legacy, as half of the county's clothing factories were located near Emmitsburg and Thurmont. Union Manufacturing expanded into these communities, but their additional facilities were closed by 1926 and 1928, respectively.

Just as changes faced the manufacturing sector, the educational sector also shifted following the Civil War. Before it, types of education in the state varied between different counties and school districts, the Maryland Constitution of 1867 created the first unified state system of public education. New public schools continued to form. Mount Airy opened its first public school in 1868 in the basement of the Ridge Presbyterian Church and Ridgeville opened its first public school in 1870. Mount Airy got its first dedicated school building in 1894. The number of high schools in the county also increased. Middletown got its first high school in 1887, which offered instruction through eleventh grade. The first public high school in Frederick for girls, Girls' High School, opened in 1889 on East Church

✧ *The Emmitsburg region hosted a range of industries. In this photograph, four employees from a broom factory pose with their products.*

✧ *The students of Girl's High School parade down Market Street during a patriotic review.*

✧ *The main building of Mercersburg College's Frederick "female department" in 1907, which once housed the Frederick Female Seminary and was later renamed Winchester Hall.*

✧ *Students in a chemistry class in Winchester Hall, c. early twentieth century.*

Street. Girls' High School offered a range of courses, including algebra, Latin, literature, drawing, and modern and medieval history. It became Frederick's first co-educational school when it was converted to a grade school for boys and girls in 1922. Girls' High School's counterpart, Boys' High School, opened in 1891 on North Market Street. It moved numerous times, eventually becoming Elm Street School, a co-educational high school. Frederick was not the only community to see an expansion of high school, and by 1914 there were eleven high schools in the county, five of which were accredited. The others only had three grades and were too small for evaluation by the state. In these high schools, girls were required to take domestic science and boys were required to take manual training. Classes were offered nine months out of the year for whites, while African-American schools were only open seven-and-a-half months a year, with similar requirements in coursework for boys and girls.

One of the county's most distinctive schools opened shortly after the Civil War, when the Revolutionary War-era Frederick Town Barracks and the surrounding grounds were set aside by the state of Maryland to make a school for deaf students. The Maryland School for the Deaf was incorporated in 1867 and opened with thirty-four pupils in 1868. Students were initially taught trades: boys were taught cabinet making, shoe repairing, and printing and girls were taught dressmaking and housekeeping. Students were also taught reading, writing, and arithmetic. The school expanded throughout the twentieth century with new buildings and additional land, eventually opening an extension in Columbia, Maryland. The Maryland School for the Deaf remains an important educational facility in the early twenty-first century and its presence has led to a thriving and vibrant deaf community in Frederick.

Another major educational institution in Frederick County originated in the late nineteenth century when, in May 1893, the Potomac Synod of the Reformed Church leased the Frederick Female Seminary buildings as part of an effort to relocate the "female department" of Mercersburg College below the Mason-Dixon Line. As part of the leasing agreement, the Frederick Female Seminary required the synod's women's college to carry out the seminary's original educational mission. Classes began that September. With an expanding student population, Margaret Scholl Hood helped the college acquire farmland west of Frederick in 1897. This expansion was well-timed as by 1898 the college was outgrowing its existing buildings, which included seven buildings in downtown Frederick. The curriculum included a range of courses in the sciences and arts, including astronomy, sociology, and philosophy. In honor of the woman who enabled the college's expansion, the institution was renamed Hood College in May 1913. The college expanded during the early twentieth century. This expansion allowed the college to sell one of the downtown buildings, Winchester Hall, to Frederick County in 1930. This building continues to house the county's government. In 1939, Hood College was freed from its obligations to the trustees of the Frederick Female

✧ *The main building at the Maryland School for the Deaf, which was demolished in the early 1960s.*

✧ *Students working in the shoe repair workshop at the Maryland School for the Deaf.*

✧ *Hood College students dress up in the outside yard at what would become Winchester Hall, c. 1920s. The Loats orphanage, the home of the Historical Society of Frederick County in the early twenty-first century, is visible in the background.*

✧ *The groundbreaking for the expansion of Hood College in April 1914.*

✧ *Frederick County men at a camp in the early 1900s.*

Seminary when the seminary's charter was voided by the state of Maryland. Hood's student body shifted through the twentieth century, with its first African-American student admitted in 1964 and its charter amended to admit men in 1970, although men were not accepted as residential students until 2002. Hood expanded through the 1970s with a graduate school, new professional programs, and an adult continuing-education program added throughout the decade.

The professional services derived from these educational resources were unevenly available to Frederick County's African-American population. This included medical services, which led to the development of a network of professionals to meet this population's needs. Frederick County's first African-American doctor was Dr. Ulysses Bourne, who was born in 1873 in Calvert County, Maryland. He studied medicine at Leonard Medical College in North Carolina and received his degree in 1902. He treated both black and white patients in Frederick from 1903 to 1953 and founded Union Hospital on West All Saints Street in 1919 with Charles Brooks, another African-American physician. Union Hospital served local residents with fifteen beds for patients and operated until Frederick City Hospital added a segregated wing, named the Baker Wing, for black patients in 1928, and Bourne was the first black physician to practice there. Bourne did not restrict his activities to medicine, and he was active in social and political causes. He founded the Maryland Negro Medical Society in 1931 and co-founded the Frederick County Branch of the National Association for the Advancement of Colored People in 1943, which he served as president for twenty years. As an extension of his political activities, Bourne ran on the Republican ticket for the Maryland House of Delegates, making him the first African-American from Frederick to run for public office. Previously, a law had prevented African-Americans from running for state office. Bourne's children, Ulysses, Jr., and Isabella Blanche, also became doctors. Isabella was the first Frederick County woman to earn a medical degree. Other professionals served Frederick County's black residents, including Dr. George J. Snowball, Frederick's first African-American dentist, who ran an office on All Saints Street.

✧ *Dr. Ulysses Bourne, Jr., followed his father into the medical field and was the first African-American physician granted privileges at Frederick Memorial Hospital.*

Other professions were also segregated and separate practitioners served the African-American community. For example, Albert V. Dixon was the first black funeral director and mortician in Frederick County. The eldest of eight children, Dixon wanted to become a doctor to help people, but he damaged his eyes in an accident while chopping wood. With a career path to help the living denied to him, Dixon focused on helping others in death, passing the state funeral directors examination in 1929. With this credential, he opened a funeral home on South Bentz Street, which, like many other businesses in the neighborhood, was run out of his home. This presented a challenge in finding space for his embalming equipment. Eventually the white morticians at the Etchison funeral home on Church Street let Dixon use their facility for his services. He operated there until he retired due to health problems in 1939.

The aftermath of the Civil War not only opened up demand for professional services, but new technologies also generated specialized occupations. In the decades leading to the war, Frederick got its first practitioner of a new art form—photography. Born in 1807 to German immigrants, Jacob Byerly started a photography dynasty. In 1839, a year after he and his wife Catherine had John, their first child to survive infancy, Catherine died. Shortly after her death, Jacob moved with John to Frederick in 1841, and—as he already knew how to produce daguerreotypes—opened a photography studio in 1842. By doing so, and by training his son and other apprentices, Byerly's photography business spanned three generations and provided a pictorial view of Frederick County's history. With a photographer in town, almost anyone could have a portrait, a luxury previously afforded largely to the wealthy when portraits had to be painted. The spread of the photographic portrait was very popular in this period. This gives us a new source of visual images of a wider range of people, in a very real way democratizing the visual past. In 1849, Byerly strengthened his ties to Frederick by marrying Catherine Hauer, a niece of Frederick resident Barbara Fritchie. Two daughters were born from this union: Grace in 1854 and Harriet Quynn in 1857. According to the 1859 *Frederick Business Directory*, Byerly's studio—described as an "Ambrotype and Photograph gallery" on Patrick Street—occupied the third floor of its building. The April 30, 1862, issue of the *Frederick Examiner* announced Byerly's move to a new location on North Market Street, where he had a skylight and a gallery, which allowed for better lighting in his photographs. Byerly continued to work through the Civil War and sold his business to his son, John Davis Byerly, in 1868. Jacob lived until 1883, when he died at age seventy-six.

Not only did his son continue Jacob's business, but he embraced new technological developments to offer new photographic services to Frederick residents. John Davis Byerly lived away from home for most of his teenage years while in school at academies in Frederick and Urbana. When John was twenty-two, the Civil War broke out, giving him ample subjects for his photography. During a Confederate occupation of Frederick, John took what is likely the most famous picture from all three generations of his family's photographic portfolio: a photograph of Confederate troops marching on Patrick Street. After the war, John travelled to the South, probably to North Carolina with noted photographer Thomas Nimmo. He returned to Frederick in 1868 and purchased the family business from his father. The next year, he married Mary Markell, the daughter of prominent Frederick resident George Markell. The couple lived on Patrick Street and had three children who survived infancy: Mary Catherine, John Davis, Jr., and Charles. John continued to document important regional events, such as the devastating 1868 flood of Frederick and the 1871 cornerstone laying at the Maryland School for the Deaf. In 1890, he photographed Francis Scott Key's grave in Frederick to show Maryland congressman Louis Emory McComas that Key's grave was austere in comparison to the Confederate Memorial Monument, an act that helped lead to the dedication of Key's monument in 1898. In addition to his professional responsibilities, John also took many personal photographs. He took many pictures of his children, which documented their growth from infancy and, following the tragic death of his son John Davis, Jr., in 1891 at age nineteen, he took several pictures of his grave. To make these images, rather than the expensive daguerreotypes, John used the collodion process, a photographic method that allowed for an unlimited number of reproductions of a given image. The Byerly photographic business under John prospered, as demonstrated by the wedding announcement for his daughter Mary Catherine in 1899, which describes the Byerlys as one of "Maryland's prominent families." That year witnessed another major shift for the family as John's surviving son Charles purchased the family business.

Like his father, Charles was a product of Frederick's public schools and the Frederick Academy. He further solidified his ties to the community when, in 1902, he married Regina "Jennie" Eisenhauer, a Visitation

✧ *Garmendia de Cordoba and his sister posed for a picture, c. 1886.*

✧ *Otho Keller and a woman named Ruth (her last name cannot be read) on a stroll beside a lake, possibly near Buckeystown, likely in the early twentieth century.*

✧ *In this Byerly photograph, the staff of the* Frederick News Post *gather for a picture, c. 1919.*

✧ *Charles Byerly frequently took family photographs, such as this one, in which his assistant Luther Potts poses with Charles's son John Francis.*

✧ *In this 1894 Christmas scene, Alonzo and Emma Marsh hold their twins Clarence and Clara in front of trees decorated with toy ornaments. From a glass negative loaned by Beverly Compton, 1990.*

✧ *A group of Frederick County men on an outing in 1910.*

Academy graduate. The couple lived on the two hundred block of East Second Street and had two sons, John Francis and Charles. After decades on the third floor of the same building, the Byerly photography studio was forced to move when the building's front wall collapsed while undergoing minor renovations in 1915. Charles and his brother-in-law and business partner Thomas Chapline decided to demolish the building to make way for a new structure, which was completed in six months. The new building was also three stories tall, but was built with heavy steel beams, in case the partners wanted to add new floors following construction. The building remains a fixture of downtown Frederick in the twenty-first century at 29 North Market Street. However, the Byerly photography studio closed, as neither of Charles's sons took over its operations. When Charles died in 1944, the studio went with him; an event that marked the end of the 102-year-old photography business.

Another long-time presence in the county, the Great Frederick Fair, was still establishing its presence after the Civil War. Less than a decade old at the beginning of the war, the fair resurged after the conflict, with ten thousand visitors in 1868. These visitors saw a range of new technologies, exhibits, and spectacles, such as a hot-air balloon flight and a jousting tournament. Over the next decade prominent national figures attended the fair, including presidents Ulysses S. Grant and Rutherford B. Hayes, in 1870 and 1877 respectively, as well as the famed editor, politician, and anti-slavery advocate Horace Greely. In 1879 the fair grew to fifteen thousand attendees. During this period, one of its most distinctive features began: Children's Day, when all of the county's public schools, and many of its private ones, close and the fair offers free admission to students. This event continues today. In the early 1890s, the fair helped two of its attendees begin a new phase in their lives with the public marriage of Jacob Kanode and Ellen Graser in front of thousands by the Reverend Doctor Edmund Eschbach of the Evangelical Reformed Church. The couple then left for their all-expenses-paid honeymoon to Niagara Falls. Several Wild West shows also performed at the fair during

✧ *This postcard shows the bustling midway of the Great Frederick Fair near the turn of the twentieth century.*

✧ *The first airplane landed in Frederick before World War I on August 21, 1911. In this image, a group of young people, including numerous soldiers, celebrate the occasion.*

✧ *Innovations in aviation were popular in the United States in the early twentieth century. This image shows crowds gathered to watch a glider at the Frederick fairgrounds.*

the 1890s, which were popular spectacles in the waning days of the Indian Wars fought in the American West. The Great Frederick Fair expanded during the twentieth century and witnessed sweeping changes in the nation and in the county.

EARLY TWENTIETH CENTURY AND WWI

With a new century, new challenges faced Frederick County's residents as industries shifted, minority populations pushed for equal protection under the law, and educational opportunities expanded. In the midst of these early changes, county residents faced an uncertain geopolitical environment as World War I consumed Europe in 1914. Although the United States did not enter the war until 1917, the war directly impacted many county residents. With Germany opposing the United States in the war, many German-Americans found their loyalties questioned. For Frederick County's large German population, which predated the American Revolution, this became a major concern and some sought to downplay their heritage. For example, some local instrumental bands changed their names from German to Dutch. Many county residents fought in the war, including Robert Nicodemus, Edward Shriner, Charles Houck, and Preston Hahn. These four Walkersville residents enlisted in 1917 and served together in France. All four returned home to a multiday victory celebration that Walkersville held for its veterans. Others never returned from the war. Lieutenant John Reading Schley enlisted six days after the United States declared war. He became Frederick's first military aviator when he transferred to the U.S. Army Aero Service. He died in a flying accident in 1918. Another county resident who gave his life was Earlston Hargett, who served as a first lieutenant in the 150th Field Artillery, part of the famous "Rainbow Division." He held an advanced degree from the Wharton School of Finance at the University of Pennsylvania. While he never planned to be a professional soldier, he used his education to write eloquent letters home that became very popular, with his final two published in the newspaper. Hargett's division saw some of the fiercest fighting in the war during the American victory at the Battle of Chateau-Thierry. Hargett died fighting in France when he was twenty-six years old. County residents on the home front also participated in the war effort and some profited. For example, brothers Osborn I. and Joseph B. Price founded Price Brothers in Frederick in 1914 to manufacture electrical equipment, primarily for radios. With the beginning of the war, they began developing radio equipment for military use.

✧ *Soldiers march in a Fourth of July parade in Frederick in the 1910s.*

✧ *An Emmitsburg couple pose in front of their home with milk cans, glass jars, and bottles.*

✧ *William O. and Robert McCutcheon, the founders of McCutcheon Cider Mill.*

Even with its end, the war left many lingering effects on Frederick County. Along with residents distancing themselves from their German heritage and the development of new industries, the global influenza epidemic that emerged from the conflict touched the county. This forced the closure of the Great Frederick Fair in 1918. The war's end also led to a wave of commemorations for those who had fought and those who had died during the war. The first World War I memorial in Frederick County was the Victory Statue, which included the names of the eighty-three county residents who died as a result of the war, as well as those of two thousand who served. At the dedication ceremony in 1924, the statue was unveiled by two mothers who had lost sons in the war: Mrs. Calvin King, whose son was the first Frederick County soldier to die in the war, and Earlston Hargett's mother, Mrs. Douglass Hargett. This was the first of numerous statues dedicated to the war throughout the county, with others in Emmitsburg, Brunswick, and Braddock Heights.

Frederick County remained one of the most productive agricultural counties in the nation throughout much of the twentieth century. The county's dairy production increased and its dairy cooperatives provided milk locally and abroad in Baltimore, Washington, D.C., and Philadelphia. While the methods of dairy production further industrialized, the dairy industry let many farmers retain their rural lifestyles. This industrialization occurred in the creameries that formed in local communities. Frederick alone contained the White Cross Milk Plant—which had easy access to the B&O Railroad—the Nicodemus Ice Cream Company along Carroll Creek, and the Excelsior Sanitary Dairy.

Although the dairy industry expanded, every Frederick County industry did not thrive in the twentieth century. Regional distillers continued producing alcohol from the county's agricultural produce and new operations were established, including J. D. Ahalt's Pure Rye Distillery near Knoxville, the Mountain Spring Distillery in Gapland, and the Outerbridge Horsey Distillery near Burkittsville. However, during the United States' prohibition of alcohol from 1920 to 1933, the distilleries suffered, and Frederick County's liquor production never recovered to pre-prohibition levels, although personal stills thrived in isolated regions. A raid on the Blue Blazes Still on Catoctin Mountain early in prohibition in 1929 illustrates the scale of these illicit operations. During the raid, authorities found over twenty-five thousand gallons of mash held in thirteen vats. Public concerns about illicit liquor production were even reflected in the culmination of a series of snallygaster sightings. The snallygaster, a large, flying, dragon-like creature first spotted in the region in 1909 was seen again in 1932 as reported in a series of tongue-in-cheek newspaper articles. This incident culminated on December 12 when the *Middletown Valley Register* announced the creature's death in a 2,500 gallon vat of moonshine. The vat's fumes knocked it out and the beast fell into the hot liquor, which had boiled it to a skeleton by the time prohibition agents George T. Danforth and Charles E. Cushwa arrived from Hagerstown to investigate. While the accuracy of this story is questionable at best, it may reflect the suspicion of unregulated liquor's quality, as the story suggests the creature's dissolution was caused by an extra portion of lye present in the mixture.

✧ *Jefferson Road during a major blizzard on March 8, 1932.*

In the late nineteenth century, a major expansion of the railroad industry in Frederick County occurred. In 1893 the B&O established a classification yard at Brunswick, a seven-mile-long facility where trains and train cars were reconfigured, built, and repaired. With the classification yard, Brunswick expanded as a major railroad hub throughout the first half of the twentieth century. By 1930 thirty percent of Brunswick's residents were employed by the railroad, a number that expanded to seventy percent by 1950. Unfortunately this was the height of the railroad industry in Brunswick. The switch from steam to diesel locomotives led to a reduced workforce in Brunswick, and, beginning in 1960, much of the work previously done at Brunswick was moved to Cumberland, Maryland. Railroad work characterized life in Brunswick through much of the twentieth century and this occupation left its mark on the town, which still houses a commuter rail station, a railroad museum, and an annual celebration of the railroad in October.

Industries devoted to production continued to develop in the county. In the twentieth century, Union Manufacturing used new technologies to produce new types of clothing. In 1929, the company began producing full-fashioned hosiery, a product that became so popular that in 1935 Union Manufacturing ceased making seamless hosiery. Illustrating how cutting-edge Union Manufacturing was in this sector, they worked with DuPont Industries to secretly produce the first hosiery made from Nylon, a material that DuPont had just developed. As the twentieth century continued, other clothing companies prospered and, following World War II, eleven textile factories employed almost fifteen hundred workers in the county. Only machine shops, such as the B&O facilities in Brunswick, employed more. One such textile company was Lincoln Tailoring Company, which made men's clothing on West All Saints Street from 1944 to 1954 and, notably in this period, employed many African-American women, guaranteeing them a full forty-hour work week.

✧ *Although it expanded throughout the nineteenth century, the railroad was sometimes impacted by natural disasters. In this image, men clear the railroad tracks in Point of Rocks of debris following a major flood in 1889.*

✧ *The rail statior at Brunswick.*

✧ *In this image c. 1936, Union Manufacturing employees board Blue Ridge busses outside the plant before departing for their annual trip to Tolchester Beach on the Chesapeake Bay. Blue Ridge was Frederick's first bus line, which operated from West Patrick Street in the 1920s until 1955 when Greyhound bought the line and moved the terminal to East All Saints Street.*

✧ *A meeting of the Ox Fibre Brush Company Quarter Century Club in April 1952.*

One major Frederick County company was the Ox Fibre Brush Company, which was founded in Frederick in 1887 by John Robinson. Robinson specialized in the production of matches and brushes from palmetto fibers. His factory in Frederick, named for his love of the red Devon ox, made a variety of brushes. One of his employees, Frederick native McClintock Young, invented a machine for Ox Fibre Brush that sped up the manufacturing process. The machine automated the fiber insertion process in the brushes, which had previously been done by hand. This was not the only innovation developed at Ox Fibre Brush, which patented ten brush-making machines. Ox Fibre Brush also expanded their product lines, adding scrub brushes and horse brushes to the capabilities of their location at the old Page Foundry on the southwest corner of West South and Court Streets. With more styles of brushes introduced, Ox Fibre Brush's business had doubled by the 1920s, but this production contracted during the Depression years in the 1930s. However, Ox Fibre Brush recovered along with the national economy during the 1940s and their business resurged, allowing the company to employ more than 350 workers who produced more than one thousand styles of brushes.

Another major Frederick County business was the Everedy Bottle Capper Company, which incorporated in 1923 after growing out of a bottle-capping business established in 1920 by brothers Harry and Robert Lebherz. While incor porating, Harry and Robert brought their brother William into the business and built a plant at the corner of North East Street and East Church Street in Frederick. Along with the production of bottle cappers, Everedy sold filter bags, letterboxes, can openers, and mops. With liquor prohibition in full swing, Everedy also sold home bottling equipment, which—along with their bottle cappers—found a ready market. As the company expanded, Everedy purchased an automatic plating machine, which allowed the company to produce chrome-plated hardware, including automobile radiators and bumpers. This aspect of the business expanded and by 1933, Everedy was chrome-plating a range of household goods, including skillets, utensils, serving trays, cocktail and coffee sets, and cookware. As the nation prepared for war against the Axis powers in the 1940s, Everedy modified their production capabilities to be able to manufacture war materiel. Everedy's first military defense contract was taken on in 1941 for the production of spherical floats for anti-submarine nets. Later, they invented a method to produce automatic acetylene welders for these floats. Everedy's military contracts expanded throughout World War II and eventually included landmines and grenades—of which they made two hundred thousand and two million, respectively—as well as parts for rockets and bombs. They also developed new folding fin stabilizers for rockets, making ten thousand spiral jet rockets a day, and they made a machine that automated bandage packaging for the Red Cross. With this vastly expanded output, Everedy reached their peak employment during World War II with 435 employees. Their average number of employees during peacetime was 168.

Frederick's residents found many ways to relax after work. Popular activities in almost any Maryland town of a reasonable size in the nineteenth century included community bands. One long-time band was the Yellow Springs Community Band, which was founded in 1888 following the dissolution of a larger band in Charlesville, Maryland. Granville Stull was their first director and fostered a welcoming environment for people to perform music. Many did not know how to play instruments when they joined, but learned. One such was Charles Stull, who began as a youth and eventually became the band's director in 1920, a position he kept until 1981, learning many instruments throughout this musical career. Charles began teaching in the Frederick County school system in 1914 and helped found the Brunswick High band shortly thereafter. This was not the only way his leisure activity influenced his

✧ *An Everedy employee manufacturing household equipment.*

✧ *The Woodsboro Concert Band organized in 1897. This photograph is c. 1914–1915.*

career, as he began teaching music in school in 1927. In the 1930s he promoted music in the schools by forming the first all-county band and chorus. In the 1940s, he founded an all-state band. His professional activities also linked to his personal ones, as he encouraged students to rehearse with the Yellow Springs Band and to be more involved with their communities. A 1958 article described the band's role in the community, noting that they were "synonymous with picnics, parades, country outings and community concerts." Other Frederick County community musical groups included the Frederick Chorale, the Swing Time Big Band, the Frederick Youth Orchestra, and the Frederick Children's Chorus.

The segregation of the county's African-American population continued into the twentieth century, which led to a variety of black-owned businesses in communities such as the South Bentz and West All Saints Streets neighborhood in Frederick. One was Jenk's Café, located on West All Saints Street, which had a strict dress code requiring hats and suits for men and dresses for women. It functioned as a social hub for the neighborhood. Informal gatherings to meet community needs also became institutions over time. One example of this is the Free Colored Men's Library. The library's roots were in the Young Men's Colored Reading Club of Frederick City, which was formed by Harry S. Johnson, E. Mitchell Johnson, and Benjamin Foreman and, according to their mission statement, dedicated to "the improvement of the social and intellectual condition of its members and their moral advancement and welfare." After a few years of meeting at one another's homes to share and discuss books, they established a community library in one side of a two-and-a-half story, wood-framed duplex occupied by Grace Snowden on Ice Street. In December 1915 the organization became the Free Colored Library and raised funds for books. By its first anniversary, an article stated that it was the only African-American-run library in Maryland and that it was "patronized by white and colored" people. It remained in Snowden's front room for the next fifteen years until, on March 12, 1929, the library's collection was destroyed in a fire that ravaged the structure. Although the library had started with only ten books, by the time of the fire the collection had as many as three thousand books. The Snowdens moved, but interest in establishing a new library for African-Americans persisted. In October 1932 the Frederick Civic Club called both for further support for the whites-only, segregated Frederick Free Library and "to establish a colored library in this city." The civic club had been instrumental in the establishment of the Frederick Free Library at the Young Men's Christian Association in 1918. Throughout the late nineteenth and early twentieth centuries, a wide range of businesses catered to the neighborhood's African-American residents, but ironically, Maryland's desegregation in the 1960s and 1970s led these shops to close as customers increasingly patronized previously white-only businesses.

✧ *The owner and employees of Barthlow's Old Glory Café, which was located on Market Street in 1915.*

Along with the businesses open to African-American consumers in Frederick County, many businesses were segregated in their employment practices. Lincoln Tailoring was a rare company, one that primarily employed African-American women, providing one of the best opportunities for them to work outside of domestic service in the region. Advertisements in the *Frederick News Post* for employment made clear who was eligible, such as this one from September 7, 1946:

> The Lincoln Tailoring Co. West All Saints St. Has openings For 3 colored women as operators. No experience necessary. Only steady workers need apply. Character references required. Apply Monday for interview.

Position advertisements for white workers were typically racially neutral, such as this one in *The News* on May 28, 1949, for a position with the Frederick Tailoring Company: "Help wanted: Women between the ages of 20–30 experienced as [...] Sewing Machine Operators, Pressers, Hand Sewers." This was one of many ways in which "white" as a racial category was unmarked, essentially appearing as the default race, with others specifically set apart as racially other.

The memoir of Lord Nickens, the longest-serving president of the Frederick NAACP, provides a personal view of how this type of labor discrimination manifested in everyday life. After completing school at age seventeen, he worked at Kemp's Department Store as a janitor on the third floor and in the basement, as well as doing occasional work at his employer's house. He did additional work for the store's advertising manager, including printing show cards and dressing mannequins in the store's display window. Nickens made five dollars a week doing this work, which he felt was a good wage for the time. However, one day a white woman was offended when she saw him dressing a white mannequin and complained to the owner about "that little colored boy" doing this work as it would "give him the inclination to grab white women." Later in his life as the president of the Frederick County NAACP from 1972 to 1994, Nickens and his organization successfully sued the county over permits issued to the white supremacist organization, the Ku Klux Klan, to hold segregated rallies. As the use of county money for segregated activities was illegal, the lawsuit succeeded and the county and the KKK were required to pay over one hundred thousand dollars to cover the NAACP's legal fees.

✧ *In May 1962, Pierre Bell and Arthur Hall challenged each other to swing hand over hand across the Swinging Bridge over Carroll Creek without getting wet, a game generations of Frederick's children played on this local landmark. Not shown is the risk these African-American children faced on the other side of the bridge, as Baker Park remained segregated in 1962.*

Segregation not only applied to businesses and organizations, but also to many public spaces. Baker Park in downtown Frederick provided a major recreational space for white citizens, but under segregation, this kind of park was denied to Frederick's African-American residents. To address this issue, one of Frederick's aldermen, Lorenzo E. Mullinix, pushed for the construction of a park for African Americans. The Baker family donated more than two acres for the park on South Bentz Street. It was named Mullinix Park for the alderman, who passed away in May 1930 after a lengthy illness and paralysis. The park was much smaller than Baker Park and the ground was largely rocky and sloping, but it was widely used by the community for events such as treasure hunts and ball games. Another public facility opened for Frederick's African-American residents was the Diggs Pool and Bath House in 1948, which was named for William R. Diggs, who lived on Fifth Street in Frederick with his wife Frances, his son Paul, and their four foster children. As Diggs was their long-time handyman, the Baker family requested that the pool be named for him in honor of his fifty years of service. Many years later, William O. Lee expanded on the decision to name the pool for Diggs, noting "It gives the black community something named after someone they can readily identify with and in which they can take great pride. Facilities and monuments serve as whispers from the past. For a people without a past surely has no future."

Separate schools were one of the most visible and damaging forms of segregation for black and white students. Not only did this lead to underfunded educations for African-American children, but it also kept racially different children apart, preventing them from developing mutual understandings and social relationships.

✧ *A group of African-American county residents in front of a school building. These people may be the teachers and staff for one of Frederick County's segregated schools.*

In Frederick County, African-American children were not provided an education past the eighth grade until 1920 as the closest black high school was found at Storer College in Harpers Ferry, West Virginia. That year, John W. Bruner, the supervisor of Frederick's African-American schools and the first black person to hold an official position in a public school in western Maryland, supported the opening of a segregated high school in a temporary location in Frederick. Eventually, in 1922, a permanent high school was opened for the county's African-American students: Lincoln High School. Although it finally made a high school education available to black students, they were not provided access to the same opportunities given to white students, as the school only received second-hand school supplies, including textbooks, while the county's white school got new ones.

African-American high school students were not the only ones to be denied educations. Kindergarten classes for black children did not exist until 1937 in Frederick County, although few white children had access to them either early in the century. This first black kindergarten opened on All Saints Street in the African-American Knights of Pythias Castle. The Knights of Pythias were a fraternal organization, which, like the Freemasons, had historically segregated membership, with separate organizations for whites and blacks. Many of the African-American fraternal orders were more politically involved than their white counterparts, although an interest in education was common across racial lines for these organizations. In 1947 the kindergarten was named for one of its long-time teachers, Esther Grinage.

The inequalities in educational opportunities between black and white students and their teachers produced early Civil Rights action in the twentieth century. During the first half of the century, African-American teachers received less pay than their white counterparts, which was a long-standing issue across Maryland. One black teacher in Annapolis, Howard D. Pindell, was approached by the NAACP to be a plaintiff in a case against this wage discrimination. However, in 1936, Pindell accepted the position of principal at Lincoln High School and moved to Frederick. He gave up his position in the court case before it went to trial, when it became the Maryland section of the 1954 Brown v. Board of Education lawsuit. Walter Mills took Pindell's place in the legal action alongside other plaintiffs in other states, which ultimately succeeded when the Supreme Court found that "separate but equal" status was not constitutional, leading to the end of school segregation.

Over the next few years, Dr. Ulysses G. Bourne, Sr., the president of the Frederick NAACP, and Thurgood Marshall, a Civil Rights attorney who went on to be the first African-American Supreme Court justice, selected Frederick County as a new location in the battle for equal teacher salaries. After unsuccessfully approaching the Frederick County Board of Education about the issue, the men sought a teacher to act as a plaintiff in a court case funded by Bourne, but none would accept out of fear for their jobs. Sadly, these fears were well-founded. In February 1938, nearly every African-American teacher in Frederick County signed a petition presented by Marshall to the Board of Education that highlighted the racially based wage difference and noted that it violated the Fourteenth Amendment to the U.S. Constitution, as their teaching positions were identical aside from the pay. In response, the Board of Education offered a fifty percent increase in salaries, which never materialized. The board also fired Pindell once a qualified replacement could be found. While the reason for this termination is unclear, many suspected that it was a move to intimidate the teachers in the wake of the petition. As an important school principal and the president of the Frederick County Colored Teachers Association, he was likely a leader of the push for equal pay. Pay would not be equalized for over a decade. In 1955, in the wake of the Brown v. Board of Education ruling, the paychecks for white and black teachers were found to be a different color, suggesting systematic discrimination. Seven years later, in 1962, the process of school desegregation began in the county, which was finally completed in March 1965.

Although the policies of segregation divided communities along racial lines, other institutions helped establish communities, even if temporarily. The Great Frederick Fair continued throughout the century. In 1911, the fairgrounds saw a major improvement, with the construction of a new bandstand with a seating capacity of three thousand people that overlooked a half-mile racetrack used for both jockey and harness races. Entertainment features at the fair expanded with popular vaudeville and circus acts, including trapeze performers, magicians, dancers, clowns, and trained animals from dogs and pigs to bears and elephants. Some acts changed, with horse and man-versus-horse pulls becoming tractor pulls and with motorcycle races becoming demolition derbies. Some events were ended entirely, including the baby show and the dog show, which was popular enough in 1902 to have its own pavilion and which was eventually revived by the county 4-H in 1972. Some sideshow elements, such as girlie, or hootchie kootchie, and freak shows were ended by the 1990s. In 1910 many central buildings were electrified and the Frederick

✧ *A group of men pictured with their cars in Braddock Heights.*

✧ *Along with its resort facilities, Braddock Heights's natural beauty also attracted visitors, such as these people posing at White Rock.*

✧ *The burning of the Braddock Hotel on August 13, 1929.*

railroad extended to encompass the fairgrounds. Along with its closure during World War I, the Great Depression forced the fair board to mortgage the fairgrounds in 1932, leading ninety percent of exhibitors to waive their premiums. Visitors could pay for entry with a bushel of wheat. This produce was later auctioned by the fair board to cover costs. Although both white and black county residents could attend the fair, segregation was a consideration that led to the construction of an addition to the bandstand specifically to seat African-American fairgoers. Through all these changes, the Great Frederick Fair continues to be an important seasonal event in the region in the early twenty-first century, continuing to attract and to educate thousands of county residents and visitors from abroad.

At the turn of the twentieth century, many new options for tourists in Frederick County emerged, whether they were from the region or from outside it. At this time, Braddock Heights developed as a resort destination, which was made possible by the construction of trolley lines by the Frederick and Middletown Railway Company. These industries were closely linked, as the railway company built one of the resorts on the heights. This allowed area residents to make simple day trips to the resorts, while visitors from major East Coast cities, such as Washington, D.C., Baltimore, and Philadelphia, often stayed throughout the summer in local houses or rented cottages. The Braddock Hotel, built in 1905, was a major residence for visitors, with seventy rooms, courts for tennis and croquet, and a large porch to fully experience the mountain air and the panoramic views of the valleys on either side of the heights. The food served at the hotel was sourced from the region's abundant farms and current fashions were exhibited by guests over meals and on the hotel's expansive lawn. Dinner was accompanied by dancing and music that could last more than three hours. The hotel remained popular throughout the 1920s, but a fire started in the building's boiler room and burned down the structure on August 13, 1929. With the area's popularity waning and the building only insured for roughly half of the property's value, the hotel was never rebuilt.

Hotels and beautiful ridgeline vistas were not the only attractions at Braddock Heights. An amusement park was constructed for visitors in the early 1920s. The park had many features, including a Ferris wheel, a giant slide, a miniature steam engine, pony rides, and a playground. A swimming pool was built in 1929 despite concerns that it would damage the limited mountain water systems. To make it possible, Potomac Edison accessed water from a nearby spring on the condition that the town's residents financed the pool's construction. It remained a popular part of the park through the 1960s and after, with thousands of visitors using it. As with other portions of the community's tourist industry, the park's popularity declined in the 1960s and much of it was sold.

Throughout this period, there were many other attractions for visitors to Braddock Heights. One was a dance pavilion that was constructed in the first decade of the twentieth century. Along with dancing, it contained bowling alleys and shooting galleries and, by the end of the 1930s, had expanded twice. Initially, visitors were required to dress formally, but, according to an article, "The ban on fancy dancing was lifted at the Braddock Heights Pavilion by R. Frank Heck, new floor manager, and patrons were expecting to tango and turkey trot into full swing. The manager yielded to the public demand for new steps, but said they would be carefully watched." Throughout the first half of the century, the dance pavilion was very popular and brought in many famous acts, including Glen Miller, Buddy Murrow, and Guy Lombardo. Another popular Braddock Heights attraction was the Braddock Heights Theater, which often held religious services and lectures and showed various silent films. It was also the home of the

✧ *County residents and visitors used trolleys such as this Frederick Railroad Company trolley to travel to Braddock Heights from Frederick. Admiral Winfield Scott Schley—a Frederick native famous for defeating the Spanish fleet at Santiago during the Spanish-American War in 1898—visited Middletown with family and friends in this private trolley car.*

✧ *Along with regional transportation, trolley lines were also used for local travel, such as this trolley that ran on Patrick Street.*

✧ *The annual outing of the employees of Kauffman's Garage to Derr's Woods on July 23, 1937.*

✧ *Richfield Mansion, the birthplace of Admiral Winfield Scott Schley, was destroyed by high winds during a hurricane in 1929.*

✧ *Braddock Heights had a number of attractions throughout the first half of the twentieth century, including this skating rink.*

Frederick Baptist Convention each summer, which attracted six hundred people. Following a lapse in use in the 1930s, the theater's owner began to operate the structure as a home for the Braddock Heights Theater group, which opened in 1939. The troupe operated seasonally, performing a different play each week throughout the summers, with ten to twelve plays each year. After declining attendance in the 1950s, the theatre closed in 1961. Although the dance pavilion and the theater operated for much of the twentieth century, Braddock Heights's popularity as a resort community suffered during the Great Depression and due to changing transportation patterns as the automobile eclipsed the rail as the primary means of travel.

WWII

As another war ravaged Europe, Frederick County again took an active role in global events. Its citizens served both in the war and on the home front. With its proximity to Washington, D.C., Frederick County saw many of its public lands used by the federal government for the war effort. Camp Ritchie, which had been established on the former site of the Buena Vista Ice Company in 1927, was taken over by the U.S. government in 1941. It was used as the Military Intelligence Training Center, a facility that offered a variety of courses for soldiers, including immersion courses in language, interrogation, and infiltration in enemy territory. After World War II, Camp Ritchie was repurposed for the Cold War by the Department of Defense. It was turned into a series of bunker retreats, later becoming the U.S. Army Seventh Signal Command headquarters. Other public facilities were used during the war by the government. In 1942 and 1943, the Great Frederick Fair was closed so that the fair pavilions could be used to store automobiles frozen by the Office of Price Administration, who rented the space. Mount Saint Mary's College also became involved in the war

✧ *Camp Frederick held German POWs during World War II.*

✧ *Elmer Wolf takes part in a shooting competition held in Foxville, c. 1936. Elmer won a watch with a stag engraved on the back while the winner, a Gettysburg man, won a 900-pound steer.*

✧ *Following World War II, Frederick County's veterans remained active in their communities, often through organizations such as the VFW. Civic and fraternal organizations saw an upsurge in membership during the post-war years.*

effort in 1941, after facing dropping enrollment numbers. They opened a CAA-War Training Service School for military aviators. From 1943 to 1944 the school also opened a Navy V-12 deck officers school, which brought almost four hundred men to the campus. In 1946 the school was presented with an anti-aircraft gun from the USS *Detroit*, which had taken part in the defense of Pearl Harbor, to honor their military training programs.

Along with education, Frederick County's extensive agricultural sector also made accommodations to produce during the war. In 1944, with a large portion of their labor pool serving in the war effort, at home and overseas, county farms and canneries were concerned about their ability to generate and package their products. Local agricultural interests noted the presence of thousands of German prisoners of war held near Laurel, Maryland, and formed the Frederick County Agricultural Cooperative Association to exploit this resource. Although many local residents raised concerns about the presence of these prisoners, the association acquired an abandoned CCC camp near Route 40 to house them. This facility became PW Branch Camp 6, or Camp Frederick, and was the only Maryland POW camp completely funded by civilians. The camp opened officially on October 1, 1944, and the prisoners were used as labor for canneries and farms, as well as for industrial operations such as quarries. Prisoners were paid hourly and retained eighty percent of their earnings, with the remainder paid to the U.S. Treasury, and as many as four hundred POWs participated at a given time. A second camp in Frederick County, Fort Ritchie, held two hundred prisoners for a similar program. By 1945, an educational component was added to the program, one intended to convince the prisoners of the benefits of American culture and democracy, as well as to teach them English. While period accounts of life at the camp are limited, stories told by former prisoners in the years after the war were generally positive, with many sharing details of extra food, spare clothes, and occasional cigarettes or alcohol shared by the farm families they worked for. One local farmer, Harold Stuff, in a story in the August 30, 1979, *Frederick News*, described sharing food and "booze" with prisoners, as well as briefly relating an incident in which a guard beat a pair of troublesome prisoners with his rifle butt. Another episode occurred on December 26, 1944, when prisoners claimed an extra day off for the Christmas holiday, citing German practice, and they were punished with a day on bread and water rations. One prisoner, Erich Pahlow, when visiting the region in the 1980s to see a Buckeystown farm he had worked on, recounted how he had operated a small artist's studio from the barracks, even producing paintings for Frederick County residents, a memory that was recounted in an article in the *Frederick News* on July 30, 1980. Even as early as January 8, 1949, when a letter from a former German POW was reprinted in the *Frederick Post*, former prisoners were contacting county residents. Peter Muetzel wrote to wish the county's residents a merry Christmas, to apologize for an escape attempt at Camp Frederick, and to update them on his life in England, where he had elected to stay after the war as his original home was in the Soviet-occupied portion of Germany.

Also on the home front, many women entered the work force, taking over jobs left open by men who were overseas during the war. This resulted in a general trend as people left rural parts of the county to work in the region's urban industrial centers. Many of the county's industries were involved in the war, such as Everedy, although many other companies entered into manufacturing for the war. Continuing the production of radio and other electrical equipment they had begun prior to World War I, Price Brothers expanded to supply the U.S. military forces with electrical and mechanical war materiel. For their efforts, they received the Army-Navy Production Award. Frederick's Muse Tailoring Company also joined the war effort by converting their facility to producing military overcoats. Given the increased production this required, their employees adjusted to these demands through piecework and overtime.

✧ *A speaker at the Everedy Company Army Navy E Award presentation ceremony on October 19, 1943.*

With the war's end and the return of the troops, Frederick County was again the site of a large celebration, one of vast scope that echoed those at the end of other wars. This occurred on September 3, 1945, when over thirty thousand spectators flooded the streets of Frederick in commemoration of victory in Europe and in the Pacific. The main event of the day was a huge parade of veterans, in which roughly 3,500 people participated, including members of the Women's Army Corps. For a county that was as central to the war effort as Frederick County, this was an appropriate and spectacular event.

Over the next decades, the county became enmeshed in a new conflict, a struggle of competing political and economic ideologies that threatened to bring the world to the brink of nuclear annihilation. Frederick County housed some of the contingency plans in case this cold war went hot.

COLD WAR AND LAST HALF OF THE TWENTIETH CENTURY

By the middle of the twentieth century, public sector jobs at the state and federal levels became major sources of income for Frederick County residents at the various military facilities and state parks in the region. The main source of these jobs was, and in the early twenty-first century continues to be, the biological research facility at Fort Detrick. Originally Detrick Field, the city's municipal airfield, the facility had served as a federal emergency airfield and training camp since 1929. As World War II began, new military threats were perceived and, by 1943, the facility was being used for biological warfare research. After the war, this research increased as biological warfare research shifted from the factory to the laboratory level. By 1950, Camp Detrick was the primary biological warfare research facility in the United States, operated by the U.S. Army Chemical Corp's Research and Engineering Division. General McCauliffe, the head of the Chemical Corps, suggested in a February 2, 1950, interview with the *Frederick News* that U.S. stockpiling of and research into biological agents prevented the Axis powers from deploying biological weapons in World War II. One major component of this research, performed from 1955 to 1973, was Operation Whitecoat, in which over two thousand volunteers from the military draft were knowingly exposed to dangerous and sometimes potentially deadly biological agents during tests at Fort Detrick. When approached about these experiments, candidates were briefed on the risks associated with the tests, as participation required informed consent from volunteers. Given this, roughly twenty percent of potential participants declined the program, and those who participated could quit at any time. Many participants were members of the Seventh-Day Adventist Church, who avoided combat duties due to religious prohibitions against killing. Many Adventists saw this testing as a form of medical missionary work, although some participants questioned the use of these tests to develop offensive weapons. During testing, volunteers entered a million-liter sphere, called an eight ball, in which scientists aerosolized biological agents for volunteers to inhale. After this, the effects of the biological agents were observed as volunteers were quarantined and treated for diseases such as Q and Rocky Mountain spotted fever, tularemia, and the plague. Although the program was designed to develop weapons, many vaccines emerged from the tests as scientists followed the full progress of the diseases and developed countermeasures. While there is no record of any volunteer dying during the tests, hundreds were made ill and, as follow-ups with participants have been limited, any long-term health ramifications are not fully understood.

This highly specialized work brought skilled professionals from all over the United States and the world, which increased Frederick County's diversity. However, following a decade of increased concerns over military bioweapons research and protests over the issue, including a vigil held by protesters from thirty-five states outside Fort Detrick, President Richard Nixon ended the production of biological weapons in the United States with an executive order. While this order continued to allow research on weaponized biological agents and into defensive measures against them, it resulted in the destruction of U.S. biological weapons stockpiles and the loss of over two thousand research positions. The speech announcing this policy shift was given by Nixon at Fort Detrick.

Research on many deadly toxins and pathogens, as well as drugs, continues at the facility. One of the most infamous tests at Fort Detrick involved experiments linked to the CIA during the 1950s with the psychological effects and possible uses of LSD, a hallucinogenic drug. One researcher on this project, Frank W.

Olson, fell from a New York City hotel window after ingesting the drug nine days earlier. After a 1994 exhumation found possible evidence of violence before the fall, controversy still surrounds the circumstances of Olson's death. Other high-profile research includes studies on anthrax throughout the 1990s and 2000s. The anthrax mailed to U.S. politicians following the September 11, 2001, terrorist attacks were traced back to a test tube held at Fort Detrick. While federal prosecutors named a Fort Detrick scientist, Bruce Edwards Ivins, as the sole culprit of the attacks following his accidental death in 2008, some aspects of this accusation have been cast in doubt. The National Academy of Sciences noted in a 2011 report that there was not enough evidence to know that the anthrax spores were from Ivins's lab. With its secret programs and elaborate safeguards, Fort Detrick remains not only a key component of American biosecurity, but also a primary economic force in Frederick as one of the city's largest employers.

Another internationally famous government site in Frederick County is Camp David, the presidential retreat within Catoctin Mountain Park near Thurmont. The camp was built from 1935 to 1938 as a Works Progress Administration project under the New Deal for the use of government employees and their families. Since then, it has gone by a variety of names, first as Hi-Catoctin, before being renamed Shangri-La in 1942 by President Franklin D. Roosevelt. The facility received its current name from President Dwight D. Eisenhower, who named it for his father and grandson. Officially, the site's name is Naval Support Facility Thurmont and it is staffed primarily by the military. Every U.S. president since FDR has used the camp during his term, and it has been used both recreationally and practically. Many of the more important and famous events at Camp David occurred when it was used diplomatically. Its remote location, which is not disclosed on maps of Catoctin Mountain Park, allows it to host famous international visitors in a relaxed setting. Many foreign dignitaries have met with sitting presidents there, including Indonesian President Suharto, British prime ministers Margaret Thatcher and Tony Blair, and Russian President Vladimir Putin. The site lent its name to two famous incidents in U.S. interventions in Middle Eastern diplomacy. In September 1978, thirteen days of secret meetings brokered by President Jimmy Carter resulted in the signing of the Camp David Accords between Egyptian President Anwar al-Sadat and Israeli Prime Minister Menachem Begin. These accords attempted to resolve the position of Palestinians within Israel and to broker a peace between Egypt and Israel, which led to Israel's withdrawal from the Sinai Peninsula. Over two decades later, in July 2000, President Bill Clinton used the site to host the Camp David Summit, a meeting between Israeli Prime Minister Ehud Barak and Palestinian Authority Chairman Yasser Arafat. The summit was another attempt to resolve the status of Palestine and to end its conflict with Israel. However, following fourteen days of negotiations, no agreement was reached and the summit ended when Arafat withdrew.

✧ *Pedestrians at the corner of West Patrick and North Market Streets in 1968.*

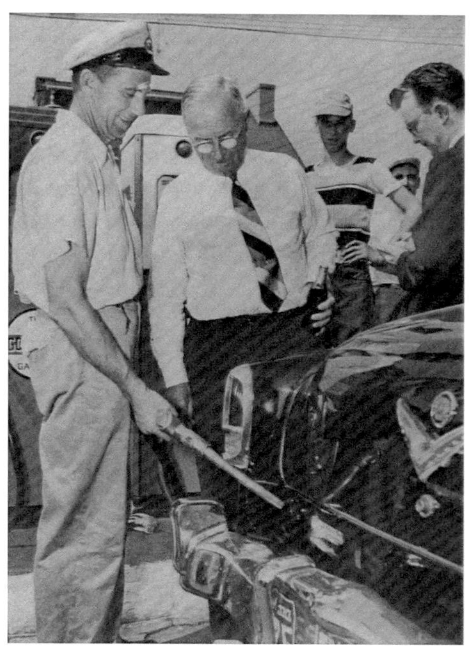

✧ *After his presidency, President Harry S. Truman passed through Frederick. This image shows Truman stopping for gas at Carroll Kehne's Gulf station on Patrick Street.*

While the World Wars, segregation, and the increasing industrialization of the region present a rigid and often grim picture of the twentieth century, the texture of daily life was also colored with moments of relaxation and recreation. For boys, little league baseball provided a popular leisure activity during much of the century. Both the National and American little leagues were present in Frederick as part of Little League, Inc. East Frederick had its first little league season in the spring of 1958, which was organized by Roy L. Main, Gene Romsburg, and John W. Turner. The league met at a ball field across Maryland Avenue from the Frederick Fairgrounds and often competed against other little league teams, such as one run by the Optimist Club. In 1962, the league's president George E. May, Sr., established the East Frederick Little League as an official Little League, Inc., franchise. With this wider visibility, they established their own field on

✧ *Frederick residents playing baseball, c. 1950s.*

West Seventh Street in 1970. Although now located in west Frederick, the name was retained as the East Frederick Little League. Fire destroyed their building in December 1997, but the team continued to play and, with declining participation, merged with Frederick's American Little League in 2006 for interleague games.

Adult baseball clubs existed in Frederick County as early as the late 1800s. Clubs played against each other, as well as against teams from other cities in the region, including Thurmont, Middletown, Emmitsburg, and Yellow Springs. The first semi-pro team in Frederick was organized in the Sunset League in 1908, playing teams from states as distant as Nebraska and Tennessee. A later Frederick team, the Hustlers, was organized in 1915 in the Blue Ridge League, which was later purchased by Major League Baseball. The Hustlers became the Warriors, a farm team for the Cleveland Indians. Not only did the newly renamed team have an initial losing record, but the local players were replaced by more professional players, leading to unrest among the fans and falling ticket sales. By 1931, the team folded, but the Hustlers were not finished yet. In 1934, the team returned in a reborn Blue Ridge League, which only lasted a year, but the Hustlers remained as an independent team. The current Frederick team, the Frederick Keys, is part of the Carolina League and moved to Frederick in 1989 from Hagerstown, where they were called the Suns. They are a major affiliate of the Baltimore Orioles and play in Grove Stadium, which was constructed to attract them. They played their first season in McCurdy Field, which was constructed for the Hustlers in 1924, linking them to the long history of baseball in Frederick.

CONCLUSION

From the eras before European Contact to the early twenty-first century, Frederick County's residents have lived on major routes connecting east and west; north and south. Living on a geographic and cultural crossroads, the residents of the region have experienced conflict and cooperation; privation and prosperity. Through war, segregation, and radical economic and social changes, they have found new ways not only to survive and make their livings, but also to struggle for change within their communities and even to find time to relax and enjoy time with friends and family. In the twenty-first century, Frederick County continues to be defined by its borders and routes, whether literal or metaphorical. While changes always reshape human relationships with other people and with landscapes, the county remains a growing and vibrant part of Maryland, from the towns and cities such as Frederick, Brunswick, and Middletown strung along the old National Road, the new interstate highways, and the railroad to communities like Emmitsburg and Thurmont that host visitors to national parks that thrive due to the county's natural beauty. Frederick County's inhabitants—whether fresh transplants or the scions of multi-generational families—continue to treasure the past and to build their lives in a place that is a national crossroads for people, ideas, and history; a border region that connects more than it divides.

✧ *Frederick County children enjoy a winter snow to ride sleds.*

Special Thanks to

Delapaine Foundation, Inc.

Hampton Inn Frederick

MedImmune Frederick Manufacturing Center

Millennium Financial Group, Inc.

Morgan-Keller Construction

SAIC-Frederick, Inc.

Sharing the Heritage

Historic profiles of businesses, organizations, and families that have contributed to the development and economic base of Frederick County

Delaplaine Foundation, Inc.

Delaplaine Foundation has awarded $8 million in community enrichment grants through 2012, since its inception in 2001, perpetuating a deeply rooted principle of giving back to the Frederick community that was born more than a century ago.

This family commitment to community enrichment began with William T. Delaplaine, who founded a commercial printing operation in 1880 in partnership with Thomas Schley. The printing operation, incorporated in 1888 as The Great Southern Printing & Manufacturing Company, eventually became the parent company for an extensive network of a newspaper and cable companies. When these properties were sold at the height of their value and success in 2001, a portion of the proceeds provided the initial funds for creation of Delaplaine Foundation.

Early home of The News *with inset of founder William T. Delaplaine as captured by artist Florene B. Ritchie.*

It was the mission of the Great Southern companies to be the dominant provider of information and communications services, while fostering a sense of community and providing customers with quality products and peerless service. The origin of Delaplaine Foundation is an inspiring story of how the dissemination of news, information, entertainment and technology—built over a span of 120 years—resulted in the creation of a foundation dedicated to the enrichment of communities and families throughout the region.

Delaplaine family members were early settlers in the area and one of the ancestors, John Thomas Schley, is credited with building the first house in Frederick. William T. Delaplaine, who founded the print shop, had a well-earned reputation for helping others. His combination of business acumen and philanthropic endeavor evolved into a heritage that has been passed down from generation to generation over the decades.

William Delaplaine, who had opened the print shop with Schley, saw newspapers as another means of selling more printing. As a result, the first issue of *The News* was printed on October 15, 1883. The newspaper prospered and, by 1888, *The News* had moved to the second floor of 44 North Market Street, where it remained for twenty-eight years.

The first issues of *The News* cost one cent or $2.50 per year delivered in Frederick City or County. The newspaper's creed, which continued through subsequent generations of the family's leadership, included these guiding principles, "to aim at thoroughness and reliability…a careful selection of general reading…our course in politics shall be neutral…with a simple record of events…we open our columns to the public and would be glad to publish anything that might be of interest to the general reader."

In the late 1880s, *The News* hosted a demonstration of the first incandescent light bulb for a group of influential local businessmen. The business leaders were impressed and the demonstration soon led to electric lights on the streets of Frederick and construction of a plant in 1892 to provide electricity to homes and businesses. This was followed in 1896 by an electric trolley system which revolutionized travel in the city.

On December 10, 1910, *The Frederick Post* was begun and the two newspapers were combined under the same ownership in 1916. *The News-Post* sponsored the appearance of the first airplane to fly in the sky over Frederick County. The event was staged before a large crowd at the Frederick Fairgrounds and helped boost enthusiasm for the daring new field of aviation.

Delaplaine was a tireless entrepreneur and, even before his printing ventures, he had invented the Peerless Paper Meat Sack. The Peerless Sack was used by local farmers for curing hams after the fall butchering. The Peerless continued to be sold through the newspapers and in area country stores for more than a century and many local farmers would never dream of curing their hams by any other method.

Unfortunately, this desire to be of service to others cost Delaplaine his life at an early age. During a severe winter in 1895, Delaplaine spearheaded a drive to collect food for the needy. He contracted pneumonia while distributing the food donations and died at the age of thirty-five. Fortunately, he was survived by four sons who shared his commitment to the community and continued to expand the family businesses as well as his philanthropic endeavors. Sons Robert, William and George, Sr., each served as president of the company during their lifetimes. The youngest son, the Honorable Edward S. Delaplaine, retired as court of appeals judge and served as chairman of the board until his death at age ninety-five in 1989. Edward was also a noted author and local historian.

In the early 1960s, few people understood the concept of cable television. However, George B. Delaplaine, Jr., grandson of William, was a visionary who understood the unlimited possibilities of this new method of communication and distribution of TV signals. Frederick Cablevision was incorporated in 1966 and opened its first office at 105 North Market Street with only five employees.

Actual distribution of television signals over a modest cable network began in 1967, providing access to twelve channels. By the end of 1967, more than 400 subscribers were being served by the new technology.

Expansion over the years resulted in several relocations of the offices and, in 1971, the cable operations were moved into a larger office at 200 East Patrick Street, then the home of *The Frederick News-Post*. In 1983 the cable office and its growing staff of twenty employees moved to 244 West Patrick Street.

Public acceptance of cable was overwhelming and, in 1977, Great Southern acquired the assets of Regional Cable Corp. in York and Adams County in Pennsylvania and named the operations GS Communications, Inc. In 1978 the company purchased the assets of C/R TV Cable, extending the operations to Charles Town and Jefferson County, West Virginia.

The company continued to grow in 1993 with the purchase of United Telesystems, Inc. of Culpeper, Virginia, and in 1995 with the acquisition of the assets of TeleMedia Corporation and Pennsylvania Classic Cable in south-central Pennsylvania.

In 1986 the cable company operations moved to a central headquarters at 442 West Patrick Street where a central call center dispatched calls for all systems and the collective cable operations of The Great Southern Printing & Manufacturing Company were operated under the name GS Communications, Inc.

With the addition of pay-per-view programming to its basic channel offerings, GS Communications offered a local origination channel—Channel 10—that broadcast from an in-house cable production studio and was used for local government and educational programming.

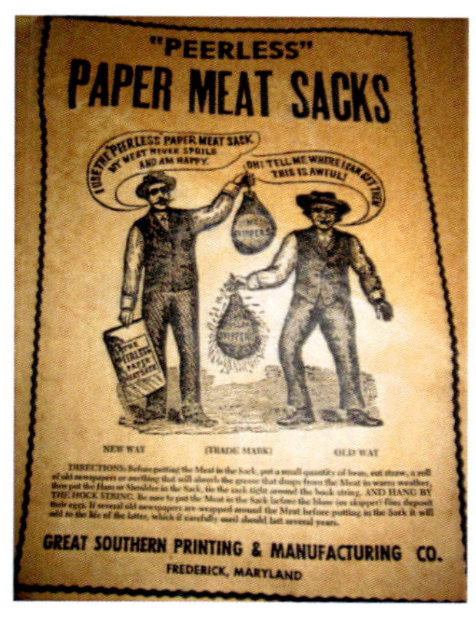

✧

Above: A Peerless paper meat sack manufactured and sold for more than a century.

Below: Home of The Frederick News-Post *from 1967–2008.*

Bottom: Corporate headquarters of GS Communications, Inc., from 1986–2001; also The Job Shop of The Frederick News-Post.

With the implementation of fiber optics and advances in broadband technology, GS Communications was listed in the top 100 MSO's (Multiple System Operators) in the United States by 1995 and by 2000 was listed in the top 35 MSO's. At the time of its sale to Adelphia in 2001, the cable company had grown to more than 123,000 subscribers in four states.

Meanwhile, advances in technology, coupled with demographic changes triggered by construction of Interstate 270, were bringing about major changes in the newspaper business. Offset printing and computerized production technology forced newspapers to abandon manually operated Linotype machines in favor of new production equipment that led to total digitized/computerized operations.

A competing newspaper was established in 1910 and was purchased by *The News* a few years later. At that time, all printing was consolidated in a facility in the first block of North Court Street. In 1967 the newspaper operations were moved to the 200 block of East Patrick Street, the former home of the first trolley company in Frederick. The newspaper was published from this location until 2008 when the Randall family, who had purchased the paper in 2001, moved it to its current location at 351 Ballenger Center Drive.

At the height of its newspaper, cable, commercial printing (The Job Shop) and Internet operations (GS Net.Works), the companies of The Great Southern Printing & Manufacturing Company employed a staff of 435 persons. Newspaper circulation at its peak was 44,444 subscribers. Cable subscribers totaled 123,000.

Above: The original Mountain City Mill property, now home of the Delaplaine Visual Arts Education Center, the former warehouse of The Frederick News-Post.

Below: Goss Urbanite Offset Press used from 1967 to 2008 as depicted by artist Ann Snyder.

In the spirit of enriching quality of life, George B. Delaplaine, Jr., spearheaded the family's donation of the Mountain City Mill building to the City of Frederick for establishing the Delaplaine Visual Arts Education

Center. Educational excellence was also promoted with the founding of the FNP History Bee in 1998 as an annual competition for Frederick County elementary students with a focus on local history and Newspapers in Education, a county-wide educational initiative. Also in the interest of promoting the arts, military band concerts were sponsored through *The Frederick News-Post* with free admission to the public. These concerts were a great success and became a widely attended tradition for many years.

Leadership and philanthropy being defining qualities, George, Jr., in addition to heading up the newspaper and cable companies, also served on many community and civic boards, including the Boy Scouts, culminating in the establishment of the annual George B. Delaplaine Distinguished Citizen Award, and State and Regional Emergency Medical committee service for nearly forty years. He was named Maryland's Master Entrepreneur of the year in 1999. Further testament to passion for the arts and education, George and Bettie Delaplaine funded the Delaplaine Fine Arts building on the campus of Mount Saint Mary's University.

The Delaplaine family has always believed in the importance of being good corporate citizens and serving as benefactors to the community at large. In an effort to maintain and sustain this benevolent philosophy, Delaplaine Foundation, Inc. was incorporated in 2001.

Chairman of the board of the Delaplaine Foundation is George B. Delaplaine, Jr.; president is Marlene B. Young; vice president is Elizabeth (Bettie) Delaplaine; George B. Delaplaine III, serves as secretary; and Philip W. Hammond is treasurer. The trustees are George B. Delaplaine, Jr.; his wife, Bettie; their sons George B. Delaplaine III, James W. Delaplaine, Edward S. Delaplaine II, John P. Delaplaine; Marlene B. Young and Philip W. Hammond.

The Foundation awarded its first official gifts in 2002, only one year after it was established. Since its inception, Delaplaine Foundation has distributed approximately $8 million through grant funding and endowments to more than 150 charitable causes and qualified 501(c)3 nonprofit organizations whose missions are closely aligned with that of the Foundation. The Foundation has been a major factor in providing lead and sustaining gifts to The Delaplaine Visual Arts Education Center and The National Museum of Civil War Medicine.

Looking to the future, Delaplaine Foundation, Inc., will continue to perpetuate community generosity and actively carry out the strong philanthropic philosophy that has been consistent with the name Delaplaine in Frederick County, the State of Maryland, and beyond.

For more information about Delaplaine Foundation, please visit their website at www.delaplainefoundation.org.

✧

Above: Officers of Delaplaine Foundation: George B. Delaplaine, Jr., founder/chairman; Elizabeth (Bettie) B. Delaplaine, vice president; George B. Delaplaine III, secretary; Marlene B. Young, president, and Philip W. Hammond, treasurer.

Left: Delaplaine Foundation Executive Committee: Philip W. Hammond, treasurer; Marlene B. Young, president; George B. Delaplaine, Jr., founder/chairman.

SERVICE GLASS INDUSTRIES, INC.

Service Glass Industries of Frederick, Maryland is a true American success story. Through determination, ingenuity, and a willingness to take risks and change with the times, a small glass company specializing mostly in residential projects and auto glass has evolved into a major firm, providing aluminum and glass materials for installation on commercial projects throughout the region.

In 1959, two enterprising businessmen from Pennsylvania, Alan Little and Duncan McArthur, purchased a Frederick-based glass business named Service Glass & Mirror. Little and McArthur owned similar businesses in Pennsylvania. The small company employed only eight people who worked from an office and shop area of less than 5,000 square feet located at 919 East Street in Frederick, across from the Monocacy Village Shopping Center.

Over a period of six years, Little and McArthur hired two different managers to oversee the business. However, neither manager was able to produce positive results. In 1965, Little and McArthur decided to appoint one of their Pennsylvania employees as the new manager of the Frederick business. That individual was a young twenty-four year old named Phil Rauh. Rauh had begun his employment with the Pennsylvania glass company in 1960, working in the shop doing basic tasks. Over the years he earned the respect of ownership and had worked his way up through the organization.

Rauh grew up in Austria and graduated from school at age fourteen. After graduation, he became a sheet-metal apprentice. One-and-a-half-years later, in 1956, Rauh, along with his mother and sister, moved to the United States and settled themselves in Harrisburg, Pennsylvania. He went back to school and graduated for the second time from William Penn High School in 1959.

Initially, Rauh was commuting to and from Frederick on a weekly basis. He would arrive on Monday and return home the following Friday or Saturday. Eventually, Rauh moved his wife, Erika, and two young sons to Frederick to become the full time operations manager of Service Glass and Mirror. Under his management, the company eliminated auto glass and residential glass from their business model and shifted their focus to commercial glazing.

In 1969, Service Glass and Mirror moved to a newly constructed building at 8006 Reichs Ford Road and the company name was changed to Service Glass Industries. The new facility was designed and equipped for doing commercial glass projects. In addition to more space for fabrication and storage of large window frames, an inside overhead crane was installed to unload large sheets of float glass. It was at this point in time that Service Glass completely halted the pursuit of residential projects to concentrate strictly on commercial projects. It was also at this time that Little and McArthur decided to bring in Rauh as a third partner.

Eight years later, Frederick native Steve Barger was nearing graduation from Frederick High School when he happened to see a job

✧

Above: Service Glass Industries, Inc., Maryland headquarters.

Right: Left to right, President and CEO Steve Barger and Chairman of the Board Phil Rauh.

Below: Wilmer Eye Institute, Johns Hopkins, Baltimore, Maryland.

Opposite, top: BRAC Administration Facility, Andrews Air Force Base.

Opposite, center: Halstead at Arlington.

Opposite, bottom: Constitution Square apartment building, Washington, D.C.

opening posted on the school bulletin board. Service Glass was seeking an assistant to the individual in charge of selling steel doors and door hardware. After much persistence, Barger was hired and began working in June of 1977.

Barger started in the office, but when office worked slowed, he helped out in the shop, cutting glass and doing various other shop tasks. Eventually, he moved to the jobsites to install glass. After an unusually cold winter, he realized he preferred working in the office. He was soon back indoors assisting others and quickly learned the ins-and-outs of the business and was bidding and managing projects on his own.

In 1985 the original owners of Service Glass, Little and McArthur, retired from the business and sold their remaining interest in the company to Rauh.

One of Rauh's first decisions as sole owner was to appoint Barger as the vice president of the organization. "I saw a young man who worked hard, was committed, had common sense and a drive. I knew he could handle the job. He took on more and more responsibility and I started to play more and more golf—what a deal," said Rauh. Barger emphasizes his success in the role was largely due to the expertise and support of many of his fellow employees at the time, several of whom remain with Service Glass to this day.

In the earlier days, the commercial projects consisted mostly of small shopping centers like the Seventh Street Shopping Center, or small convenience stores, such as Highs Dairy (a 7-11 type store) and even small schools.

As the size, quantity and complexity of the commercial projects grew, even more space was needed. In 1988, Service Glass relocated to Mount Zion Road where it currently operates out of a multi-building complex.

Over the years, Rauh and Barger's business relationship grew and, eventually, they became equal partners in the business. Service Glass is presently run by President and CEO Barger and Chairman of the Board Rauh.

Today, Service Glass's direct workforce includes forty to fifty men and women as well as an additional fifty or sixty individuals employed through the use of regular installation subcontractors. Service Glass has had business relationships with some of these subcontractors for decades.

Service Glass continues to work strictly on commercial projects and is a well-known and respected contract glazier for projects of all sizes in Maryland, Virginia, and the DC-Metro area. Their portfolio includes high-rise office buildings, high-rise commercial/residential buildings, hospitals, universities and large schools. Additionally, they have performed many custom art glass installations, including the "Dreaming" glass wall currently installed on the outside of what some may remember as the old Frances Scott Key Hotel building on West Patrick Street.

Service Glass is a long-standing member of Associated Builders and Contractors, a nationally recognized builders association, whose Washington, D.C., and Virginia Metro chapters have six times recognized them as the 'Subcontractor of the Year' in their respective category. "It has always been our goal to provide our customers with a level of service that is superior in our trade. We like to think it is a primary reason for our team's success," Rauh and Barger agree.

In fifty-four short years, Service Glass has transformed itself from a small division of Harrisburg Glass Company into a major commercial contract glazing firm known for emphasizing the 'Service' part of its name. "Though many things have changed over the years, a few things have stayed the same; hard work and commitment by our dedicated people have brought us to where we are today and will carry us into the future. Our younger staff continues to learn from our experienced staff. We hope our younger professionals will carry on the company for decades to come," says Barger.

Service Glass Industries is proof that the American dream is still alive, and with hard work and dedication, success is possible.

✧

Top: Metro Park 6 office building, Alexandria, Virginia.

Above: The "Dreaming" glass wall installed on the outside of the old Frances Scott Key Hotel building on West Patrick Street, Frederick, Maryland.

Right: Dulles Station office building, Herndon, Virginia.

PHOTOGRAPH COURTESY OF ERIC TAYLOR.

Tourism Council of Frederick County, Inc.

Frederick County faced challenges forty years ago as the nation prepared to celebrate its bicentennial. Although located less than an hour from Washington, D.C., and Baltimore, and close to hallowed Civil War ground at Gettysburg, Antietam, and Harpers Ferry, the area had much work to do if it hoped to attract the thousands of visitors expected during the country's 200th anniversary.

In the mid-1970s, historic Downtown Frederick had begun to deteriorate. Numerous utility lines and florescent street lamps lined the streets and crowns of asphalt had accumulated to the point that car doors scraped the sidewalks when visitors tried to park.

A local effort called Operation Town Action was organized to 'jump-start' an improvement program. The city began to rebuild Market Street, tearing out the roadway and sidewalks and putting wiring underground before rebuilding with attractive, classic materials. The Frederick *News-Post* helped stir enthusiasm for the project and the Historic District Commission helped preserve the town's original architecture. Frederick's first parking garage was constructed on East Church Street, followed by a visitor center next door. With the national bicentennial looming, historic buildings such as the Hessian Barracks at the Maryland School for the Deaf were spruced up.

Other historic structures were saved. Schifferstadt, a stone house considered a fine example of German colonial architecture, was scheduled to be torn down to build a gas station. A newly-formed Frederick County Landmarks Foundation managed to save and preserve the home. Another building, due to become a parking lot, now houses the Historical Society of Frederick County's Museum of Frederick County History. The era also saw establishment of the Weinberg Center in the former Tivoli Theater and, with that, the establishment of the Frederick Arts Council.

By 1976, Frederick had been designated an All-America City. In the enthusiasm surrounding the bicentennial, residents took renewed pride in the community's role in the country's history and also recognized the economic value of attracting visitors.

The Tourism Council of Frederick County, an early example of a successful public/private partnership, was spun off from the Chamber of Commerce. The organization operates with a $2 million budget, with about half coming from the Frederick County hotel tax and the remainder from private sector support and various grant sources.

In addition to the covered bridges, orchards, the Seton Shrine, Grotto of Lourdes, Brunswick Railroad Museum and the Francis Scott Key Monument, a number of new tourist attractions have been added in recent years, including the National Museum of Civil War Medicine, Monocacy National Battlefield's expansion and Visitor's Center, and the continued redevelopment of Downtown Frederick.

Visitor spending in Frederick County now totals more than $325 million annually, making tourism one of the county's top industries.

The Frederick Visitor Center is now located in a rehabilitated circa 1899 cannery warehouse, right at the gateway to historic Downtown Frederick.

For more information about tourist attractions and visitor accommodations, check the website at www.visitfrederick.org.

✧

Top: The current Frederick Visitor Center at 151 South East Street opened in April 2011 in a renovated 1899 cannery warehouse.

Above: The former Frederick Visitor Center on East Church Street welcomed more than one million visitors.

FoodPRO Corporation

FoodPRO's tradition of employee ownership and great customer service began on November 1, 1935, when FoodPRO Corporation opened as a second location for Baer Brothers of Hagerstown. The warehouse was operated by Niemann Brunk.

Niemann was joined by his brother, Milton, in 1941 and they purchased what became the Frederick Produce Company. The first downtown location was 235 East Fifth Street, the current home of the Redman's Club. In March 1951, FoodPRO moved down Fifth Street and across East Street to its current location at 321 East Fifth Street.

Above: The Brunk Brothers.

Records from 1935 indicate that the business started with assets of $617.57. Potatoes then were 50 cents for a 50 pound bag, apples were 35 cents a bushel, lettuce was 5 cents a head and a bunch of celery was also 5 cents. At this time, FoodPRO primarily sold produce to small, local general stores.

Frozen foods were added in 1945 as FoodPRO continued to service general stores and added more retail grocery stores. In March 1951, FoodPRO moved one block east to the present location at 321 East Fifth Street and added larger sizes of canned goods and related food products for the newly developing restaurant trade. FoodPRO has always been willing and capable of adapting to the ever-changing economy.

Continued growth allowed FoodPRO to add on to the Fifth Street facility in 1964 and again in 1970. In March 1974 the current two story office building was constructed on the front of the distribution facility. At the same time, new loading docks were built and warehouse space was increased. The latest several additions have increased the facility to more than 70,000 square feet of frozen, refrigerated and dry food distribution space. A new retail store, the Chefs Outlet, was built and opened to the public in 1988.

In 1997, FoodPRO became an ESOP "Employee Owned Company," with the employee retirement fund becoming the largest stockholder. This resulted in the employees feeling even more focused on providing customers with consistent quality products and memorable services.

Family matters at FoodPRO and many families have been involved in the growth and development of the employee-owned local Frederick company. Included are the Brunk family—Niemann, Milton, Jack and Scott; the Easterday family—Jimmy and Dennis; the Furbee family—Ed and Jordan; the McAteer family—Kevin and Steven; and the Coe family—Bill and Dave.

Over the years, FoodPRO has enjoyed the long term loyalty and contributions of many employees. Notable examples include Gene Morgan—51 years; Ed Blumenauer and Jimmy Easterday—50 years; Kathleen Heim—49 years; Dennis Easterday—39 years; Reds Tyeyar, Zeke Zimmerman and Don Orrison—35 years; Dave Young and Corie Wachter—34 years; and Tom Wright—30 years.

From our start in 'fresh' produce, FoodPRO has grown to become a key provider of the highest quality fresh meats, seafood and poultry, as well as dairy products, milk, cheeses, coffees and beverages. In addition, equipment and related support services are provided for the restaurants and nursing homes in our six state marketplaces. By also providing all the canned, dry and frozen foods, paper and disposable products, as well as equipment and supplies, FoodPRO essentially provides restaurants and nursing homes with anything they might need or use to prepare and provide meals. The meals you enjoy when you eat out at the many fine locally owned Frederick County restaurants most often start out in the FoodPRO warehouse on Fifth Street in downtown Frederick.

Currently, FoodPRO services more than 2,500 restaurants and nursing homes in six states with revenue of over $60 million, and all from the original downtown Frederick location. FoodPRO provides quality employment for 106 Frederick County families.

Officers of FoodPRO are Chairman Jack Brunk; President Ed Furbee; Vice President Scott Brunk; and Secretary/Treasurer Keven McAteer. The board of directors provides the leadership required for this growing employee-owned company that is proud to have started right here in Frederick in 1935.

FoodPRO's employee owners have a lot to be proud of and are very hopeful and excited for all that is ahead in their future. FoodPRO is committed to remaining a successful Frederick County employer.

Please visit FoodPRO's retail Chefs Outlet store that is open to the public and where there is no membership fee. Here you can buy restaurant-quality foods for your home, club or organization all at wholesale prices. Chefs Outlet is located at 321 East Fifth Street.

✧

Center: Left to right, Officers of FoodPRO are Chairman Jack Brunk; President Ed Furbee; Vice President Scott Brunk; and Secretary/Treasurer Keven McAteer.

Cozy Restaurant and Country Inn

The excitement of history in the making is always in the air at the Cozy Restaurant and Country Inn, where an eighty-five year old heritage of warm hospitality blends with the mystique of nearby Camp David, a retreat for the nation's chief executives since the days of President Franklin Roosevelt.

Cozy, founded in 1929, is the oldest family owned restaurant in Maryland and one of the first restaurants to be enshrined in the Maryland Restaurant Association Hall of Honor, as well as the National Restaurant Association Hall of Fame.

Cozy was started by Wilbur Freeze in the dark days of the Great Depression, when homeless men called hobos roamed the country looking for work. Freeze set up tents, established a 'camp kitchen' and offered the hobos food and shelter in exchange for work. The hobos helped build the Cozy's first cottages and a twelve stool sandwich counter. They also dug a pond in front of the cottages that still exists today and has become a local landmark.

Wilbur married Mary Gehr a couple of years after opening Cozy and the two worked side-by-side for many years, building the restaurant and inn into a popular destination, both for locals who enjoyed the delicious food and tourists traveling through the beautiful Catoctin Mountains. Wilbur and Mary's son, Jerry, operates Cozy today.

Cozy's history with the nation's presidents actually pre-dates the establishment of Camp David. In 1929, President Herbert Hoover's personal secretary, Larry Ritchie, built a retreat in the Catoctin Mountains and became a close friend of the Freeze family. A bear skin rug made from a bear killed by President Hoover was on display at Cozy for many years, and his fishing license is still on display in Cozy's Camp David Museum.

Camp David was developed as an official presidential retreat in 1942 to give President Franklin Roosevelt a peaceful place to escape from the pressures of World War II. Roosevelt named the retreat Shangri-La, a name that was retained until President Dwight Eisenhower renamed it Camp David, in honor of his grandson.

Cozy supplied the original housing for the Secret Service agents who protected President Roosevelt at the retreat. In the early years of Shangri-La, newspapers for the president and his guests were delivered to the Cozy.

Many world leaders conferred with President Roosevelt at the retreat during World War II, including British Prime Minister Winston Churchill. It was reported that Churchill liked to slip down to the Cozy for a martini and an

opportunity for a little friendly gambling in a back room.

Because of its proximity to Camp David, thousands of top government officials, White House staff members and members of the news media have been drawn to Cozy Restaurant and Country Inn over the years. It is estimated that more than twenty million people have enjoyed Cozy's hospitality, including celebrities such as Barbara Walters, Walter Cronkite, and Wolf Blitzer. The Cozy was used as the site for a network TV interview with Secretary of State Condoleezza Rice during the George W. Bush administration. Other top government officials, including David Axelrod, aide to President Barack Obama, have also been interviewed at the Cozy.

The Camp David Museum at Cozy celebrates the rich history of Shangri-La/Camp David through pictures and memorabilia of presidents from Hoover through today. The photos and artifacts in the museum have been given to Cozy since 1929 by members of the media, presidential staff members and foreign dignitaries. It is the only museum of Camp David history in the nation and also includes a souvenir and gift shop.

The Freeze family is grateful for the support of ABC, CBS, NBC, CNN, AP, MPT, AFP, UPI, White House Press Corps and Reuters Press, along with the many local and independent press organizations, and Thurmont Historian, George Wireman, without whom the Camp David Museum would not be possible.

In addition to the historic ambiance, guests at Cozy may enjoy dining at its best in one of eleven multi-personality dining rooms. From a bite to a banquet, you can enjoy Cozy's bountiful buffets or table service. The Cozy chefs use only the freshest and finest ingredients, including in-season herbs and vegetables that are homegrown and hand-picked from the restaurant's own gardens. Several showcases at the restaurants are filled with pictures, autographs and other memorabilia of those who have visited Cozy and Camp David over the years.

In addition to the restaurants, Cozy offers a friendly pub with beer, wine, and liquor and a tea room. Catering is available for as many as 3,000 people and many choose Cozy for wedding receptions or banquets.

Cozy's quaint and charming rooms and cottages are decorated to commemorate the style of the Presidents and other dignitaries who have visited through the years. The Cozy Inn offers traditional rooms and cottages, premium deluxe rooms and executive suites that include Jacuzzis and gas fireplaces.

For more information about Cozy Restaurant and Country Inn, or to make reservations, visit their website at www.cozyvillage.com.

The Cozy Inn and Restaurant closed in 2014 after eighty-five years in business.

KEENEY AND BASFORD P.A. FUNERAL HOME

✧

Top, left: The Trail Mansion.

Top, right: The Etchison family.

Below: Colonel Charles E. Trail, c. 1850.

Keeney and Basford P.A. Funeral Home, founded in 1848, is the longest, continually-operating business in Frederick County. At your family's time of need, you can depend on Keeney and Basford to care for you and your loved ones, just as we would care for one of our own family.

As a full-service funeral home, Keeney and Basford provides families with funeral, cremation, pre-arrangement and pre-funding for funerals and services.

Keeney and Basford was established 165 years ago by John Garrison Etchison. Originally called M. R. Etchison and Son, the establishment had several different locations in downtown Frederick, including East Patrick and North Market Street addresses, before moving to its current location at 106 East Church Street in 1939.

The historic building that now houses Keeney and Basford is known as the Trail Mansion. Built in 1852 by Colonel Charles E. Trail, it is a beautiful example of classic Italianate architecture. Of particular note are the front entrance area, the Italian-designed windows and marble fireplaces, and the elaborate ceilings similar to those found in nineteenth century European estates.

For nearly 125 years, the funeral home was owned and operated by the Etchison family; much of that time with the help of only one employee, Frank R. Smith. After the retirement of Marjorie Etchison and A. Hart in 1971, the firm was sold to Frank R. Smith, Donald M. Fadeley, Robert W. Keeney and Richard C. C. Basford.

The present owners, Rick Graf and Keith Roberson, are long-time Keeney and Basford employees who assumed ownership in 2007 and continue to conduct the business based on a heritage of compassion and dedication to the Frederick community.

Unlike many other funeral facilities, Keeney and Basford has made the decision to remain unaffiliated with any outside ownership or operational concern. Being family-owned and independent allows us to continue to care for your family as we always have—neighbor to neighbor, friend to friend—with sincere, superior service and outstanding compassion and care.

For peace of mind, Keeney and Basford offers pre-planning options that ease the burden on survivors during their time of bereavement. Many who have undergone the emotional strain of arranging a funeral within hours of losing a loved one have made the choice to pre-plan their own funeral. Doing so lifts the burden from their loved ones by relieving decision-making pressure at a time of grief and emotional stress.

Funeral arrangements are a deeply personal choice. Pre-planning provides the time needed to make practical, detailed decisions that reflect your standards, lifestyle, taste and budget. And it assures your family that the choices you make will be carried out as planned.

When you finalize your plan, Keeney and Basford can advise you of the total cost. You do not have to set aside funds for your plan, but doing so protects you against escalating funeral costs. By locking in today's funeral costs and ensuring that the necessary funds are set aside, you help relieve yourself of unnecessary future worry and your survivors of an unexpected expense.

The professional staff at Keeney and Basford is dedicated to the Frederick community, a concern that is made obvious through their involvement in church, fraternal, benevolent and civic organizations. Staff members are caring and experienced professionals who understand that each family is unique and has personal requests and traditions. These requests and traditions are of utmost importance to our staff of licensed funeral directors.

The current owners of Keeney and Basford continue to conduct the business based on a history of compassion and dedication.

"Rick and I consider it an honor and privilege to have taken on the ownership of Keeney and Basford, and promise to uphold its longstanding reputation for providing families with compassion, dignity and respect," comments Roberson.

Our code of behavior is simple—serve as you would be served. This is why a licensed member of our staff is on-call for you at all times, twenty-four hours a day, seven days a week. When death occurs, or when your family and friends are visiting our facility, you expect and deserve immediate answers and assistance. At Keeney and Basford, there is one thing you can always depend on; we will care for you and your loved ones at your time of need, just as we would care for our own family.

At Keeney and Basford, your family matters. For more information about Keeney and Basford P.A. Funeral Home, check their website at www.keeneybasford.com.

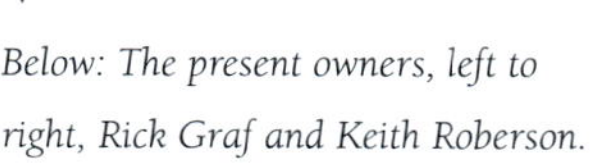

Below: The present owners, left to right, Rick Graf and Keith Roberson.

SAIC-Frederick, Inc.

SAIC-Frederick is speeding the development of new technologies and treatments for patients with cancer and AIDS. At SAIC-Frederick, a staff of scientific, technical, and support professionals conducts basic and applied research in cancer and AIDS, operates and manages the federal government's only vaccine manufacturing facilities, and runs the high-performance Advanced Biomedical Computing Center.

SAIC-Frederick, a wholly owned subsidiary of SAIC, operates the Frederick National Laboratory for Cancer Research, sponsored by the National Cancer Institute (SAIC-Frederick is soon to be renamed Leidos Biomedical Research Inc.). FNL is a federally funded research and development center dedicated to rapidly translating basic research into new technologies and treatments for cancer and AIDS. The organization develops and applies advanced technologies across a broad R&D spectrum that includes genetics and genomics, protein science, nanotechnology, bio informatics, advanced biomedical imaging and biopharmaceutical development and manufacturing.

FNL was established as the Frederick Cancer Research and Development Center in 1972 after President Nixon signed the National Cancer Act, converting some Fort Detrick labs into a leading center for cancer research. In 1975 the center was designated as a Federally Funded Research and Development Center (FFRDC).

FNL is located within the gates of Fort Detrick on property owned by the Department of Health and Human Services. A second campus is located at Riverside Research Park. FNL is a government-owned/contractor-operated facility and the operating contractor is SAIC-Frederick.

SAIC won the FFRDC contract in 1995 after a full and open competition. The contract period was 1995-2001 and the negotiated contract value was $907 million. The contract was renewed after full and open competition in 2001 with a negotiated contract value of $2.5 billion. SAIC-Frederick was awarded a ten year sole-source contract in 2008. The contract value is $5.3 billion.

FNL is the only federally funded research and development center in the National Institute of Health and Human Services and the Department of Health and is the only one in the nation dedicated solely to biomedical research. SAIC-Frederick takes on projects that cannot be accomplished by other in-house and contracting mechanisms. The contract offers flexibility and rapid response, and provides essential technologies in genetics and genomics, proteins and proteomics, integrated in vivo services, imaging and nanotechnology, advanced biomedical computing, Center for Applied Preclinical Research and biopharmaceutical development.

FNL is differentiated by three factors: first, its composition creates a collaborative research community. The Frederick National Lab contains a Federally Funded Research and Development Center, a government-owned, contractor-operated entity established to bridge the public and private sectors. Several NCI researchers and their labs are co-located near the Frederick National Lab, to better access FFRDC resources, primarily in the area of advanced technology and drug discovery. This co-location increases opportunities for collaboration, intellectual exchange and discovery.

Second, its status as an FFRDC gives FNL flexible partnering capabilities. The lab, as an FFRDC, can craft flexible and tailored partnership agreements with other government researchers and the private sector.

Finally, given its composition and partnering abilities, the lab is able to perform complicated projects that can be designed and implemented nowhere else.

FNL conducts basic, translational and pre-clinical research and development in cancer and AIDS. Investigators and technical staff at FNL collaborate with other government agencies, academic institutions, life-science companies, and nonprofit research organizations to develop the next generation of tests and treatments that will benefit families affected by cancer.

The lab has established a program through which outside organizations—including life science companies and other commercial entities—can enter directly into cooperative research and development agreements with SAIC-Frederick. These agreements can accommodate the development of new technologies for research, or for clinical applications that benefit patients.

FNL offers education, training and professional development, as well as expert consultation in quality control, regulatory affairs, and patient safety. As a national resource, FNL helps biomedical scientists form a solid bridge between basic research and clinical practice, with support that is not readily available elsewhere.

SAIC-Frederick is headquartered on a sixty-eight acre campus within the perimeter of Fort Detrick. It has business and scientific operations and subcontracts at various locations, principally in Frederick and Montgomery Counties, as well as across the country and overseas.

SAIC-Frederick's 1,850 employees are actively involved in a program of community support and outreach that touches the areas of business, education, health, charity, science and culture. A scholarship program supports high school students pursuing college studies in science, technology, engineering and mathematics. An annual employee giving campaign, offering payroll-deduction and matching contributions, raised more than $175,000 during its most recent cycle. Employees also volunteer their time to organizations such as Habitat for Humanity and the Children's Inn at the National Institute of Health.

SAIC-Frederick is a wholly owned subsidiary of Science Applications International Corporation (SAIC), a Fortune 500® company.

Morgan-Keller Construction

Above: *Morgan-Keller staff at original Wolfsville, Maryland, location.*

Below: Left to right, three generations of ownership, Gail Guyton, Ralph Morgan, Bradley Guyton and Darrell Guyton.

PHOTOGRAPH COURTESY OF TOM LESSER PHOTOGRAPHY.

The fifty-eight year history of Morgan-Keller Construction is a story of successful growth and flexibility, made possible by focusing on changing markets and client needs. During its nearly six decades in business, Morgan-Keller has transitioned from a high quality custom homebuilder to one of the region's largest and most respected commercial builders.

Morgan-Keller was founded by Ralph W. Morgan and Lawrence Keller in 1955 as a family-owned residential construction company located in Wolfsville, Maryland. Morgan handled the interiors, carpentry and office work, assisted by Keller, who looked after masonry operations. Only four people were on the payroll when the company began.

In the early days, Morgan-Keller concentrated on single-family 'spec' homes and soon completed entire developments, including Woodlea and Woodmere in Middletown and College Estates II and West Hills I and II in Frederick. An emphasis on building excellent quality homes at a competitive price helped the company grow rapidly.

Ralph Morgan's son-in-law, Gail T. Guyton, began working for the company while a college student in 1958 and joined the firm full-time in 1962 after graduating from American University with a major in business. He quickly learned the business side of the company, including the skill of estimating, purchasing and sales.

By 1965, Morgan-Keller had started doing commercial work, including pre-engineered metal buildings. Among the firm's significant projects during the 1960s and 1970s were the Boise Cascade Plant in Shippensburg, Pennsylvania; Carrolltown Shopping Center in Eldersburg, Maryland; and Fedder's Corporation compressor plant in Walkersville, Maryland. In the mid-1970s, Morgan-Keller began building retirement communities such as Homewood in Williamsport, Maryland.

Gail Guyton became president of Morgan-Keller in 1980 and his first major decision was to move away from the often-volatile field of custom residential construction and concentrate on commercial, industrial and construction management operations, including multi-family residential. Guyton purchased the company in 1981 and his son, Brad, joined the company in 1983.

With both undergraduate and graduate degrees in business from Mount St. Mary's College, Brad brought new and innovative ideas to the firm. In 1988, he started a Specialty Contracts Department and, in 1996, Morgan-Keller Concrete was created to fill an important market niche.

Darrell Guyton, Gail's younger son, joined Morgan-Keller in 1987 after graduating from Western Maryland College. He spent his early years learning all aspects of the business by working on jobsites, doing estimates and working as a project manager. In 1994, Darrell took over the Specialty Contracts Department, which handles Morgan-Keller's fast-track projects under $2 million.

Brad became president and CEO of Morgan-Keller in 1997 and his integrity, strong leadership and foresight have created a level of confidence reflected in the company slogan: "Our Reputation is Building Every Day." Morgan-Keller has successfully completed hundreds of projects in a four state region, all of which meet the same high standards set by Ralph Morgan. The company's many repeat customers, combined with its solid reputation, confirm the fact that Morgan-Keller is a skilled and expert practitioner of construction techniques and methodology.

Over the past twenty years, Morgan-Keller revenues have increased four-fold. The team member base has doubled during the same period and the company continues to expand its labor base. The company has offices in Frederick and Columbia, Maryland, and the customer base is located within Maryland, the District of Columbia, Virginia, West Virginia and Pennsylvania.

The culture of Morgan-Keller Construction includes a strong belief in giving back to the community that has given the company so much during its long history. Morgan-Keller and its team members support a long list of community projects through financial contributions, active participation and the organization of scholarships and charitable events. Morgan-Keller team members are encouraged to dress casually each Friday in exchange for a donation to one of the many local charities.

In addition, Morgan-Keller team members assist three or four local families during the holiday season by making their Christmas complete with presents and a traditional Christmas dinner.

Since 1998, Morgan-Keller has sponsored a scholarship program supporting the educational goals of Certified Nursing Assistants (CNAs) and Geriatric Nursing Assistants (GNAs) throughout Maryland.

Morgan-Keller's United Way committee organizes an annual campaign to raise funds for agencies supported by the United Way of Frederick County. Many team members donate generously to the United Way each year. In addition, Morgan-Keller organizes several blood drives for the American Red Cross each year and encourages employees to donate whenever they can.

Morgan-Keller Construction looks forward to continued growth in the mid-Atlantic region. The firm's future rests on a solid foundation of past success with both negotiated and design-build projects in a number of construction categories, including class A office, retail, senior housing, multi-family housing, educational facilities, warehouses and manufacturing, financial institutions and public sector service buildings.

✧

Above: Left to right, Ralph Morgan and Gail Guyton at West Hills II Development in Frederick, Maryland.

Below: Morgan-Keller's current Frederick headquarters located on Thomas Johnson Drive.

Mount St. Mary's University

✧

Above: Mount St. Mary's University has grown from humble beginnings in the early 1800s to a vibrant 1,400 acre campus located in Emmitsburg with a second campus in Frederick. DuBois Hall, the first residential hall on campus, was built in 1808 as an all-purpose building. Then it housed the school president, faculty and students. DuBois Hall and three other buildings now comprise the Terrace Complex, which remains a focal point of campus.

Below: Mount St. Mary's has been a leader in higher education for more than 200 years. Since its founding in 1808 to the first co-educational class in 1972, to the present, the Mount cultivates a community of learners formed by faith, engaged in discovery, and empowered for leadership in the Church, the professions, and the world. The Mount offers more than forty undergraduate majors, minors, concentrations, interdisciplinary and special programs, along with five graduate degree programs. All undergraduate students complete the Veritas Program, a common, four-year curriculum that prepares students for success in the modern world, while giving them a solid grounding in the Catholic intellectual tradition.

Mount St. Mary's University, America's second oldest Catholic institution, is dedicated to faith, discovery, leadership and community. Mount St. Mary's also includes Mount St. Mary's Seminary and the National Shrine Grotto of Our Lady of Lourdes. Mount St. Mary's is an institution of higher education for both undergraduate, graduate and seminary students.

Mount St. Mary's University and Mount St. Mary's Seminary strive to graduate men and women who cultivate a mature spiritual life, who live by high intellectual and moral standards, who respect the dignity of others, who seek to resolve the problems facing humanity and who commit themselves to live as responsible citizens.

The origins of Mount St. Mary's can be traced to 1728, when a group of Catholics seeking religious freedom left St. Mary's City, Maryland, and traveled hundreds of miles west to the Blue Ridge Mountains near Emmitsburg. Here they founded a settlement based on peace and religious freedom. In 1798 a church was established for English Catholics near Emmitsburg. That same year, St. Joseph's Church was built in Emmitsburg to serve the mostly Irish Catholic population.

Father John DuBois, the founder of Mount St. Mary's, came to America in 1791 to escape the French Revolution and was sent by his Bishop to Frederick, Maryland, twenty miles south of Emmitsburg. In 1805, Father DuBois laid the cornerstone of Saint Mary on the Hill, a church that united the English and Irish congregations. He also taught school and purchased the first parcel of land for what became Mount St. Mary's Seminary.

Also in 1805, according to legend, Father DuBois was attracted to "a light on the mountain and found a blessed spot, one of the loveliest in the world, and there erected a crude cross, the symbol of the holy work he was undertaking." This was the original grotto, which today stands as the National Shrine Grotto of Our Lady of Lourdes. The Shrine is the oldest known American replica of the French shrine and attracts 400,000 visitors to the Emmitsburg area each year.

Three years later, the Society of St. Sulpice in Baltimore closed its preparatory seminary in Pennsylvania and transferred the seminarians to Emmitsburg. Their arrival in 1808 marked the formal beginning of Mount St. Mary's. Father DuBois was appointed the school's first president.

Class records from 1811, the oldest in existence, show the school had 101 students, both collegians and seminarians.

In 1809, Elizabeth Ann Seton arrived with a small group of young women to establish a school in Emmitsburg. The Mount helped her establish the Sisters of Charity of St. Joseph's and open parish schools, including St. Joseph's Academy and Free School, the first free Catholic school for girls staffed by Sisters in the United States. This work led to Seton's canonization as America's first native-born saint.

The Right Reverend Simon Gabriel Bruté joined Father DuBois in 1812, teaching divinity and philosophy and serving as spiritual advisor to the Sisters of Charity. He remained at the Mount for twenty-five years and played a significant role in the institution's growth.

Father DuBois left the Mount in 1826 when he was named Bishop of New York. Father Bruté and Father John Purcell, who became president in 1829, obtained the first official charter for the University from the State of Maryland in 1830.

Because of the work of its clerical graduates during the school's early history, Mount St. Mary's became known as the 'Cradle of Bishops.' Mount alumni served as the first Bishops of fifteen newly formed dioceses and thirty-two dioceses in the U.S. have been directed by at least one Mount graduate. In all fifty-one Mountaineer alumni priests have been consecrated as Bishops in the Church.

From its beginning with only a few students in 1808, the Mount has grown tremendously, becoming a premier Catholic university for students in the Mid-Atlantic region.

Mount St. Mary's has two beautiful campuses. The historic main campus is located on 1,400 tree-lined acres in Emmitsburg and is home to the traditional undergraduate degree programs and sixteen Division I athletic teams. The Mount's Frederick campus is located by the FSK Mall and is home to adult undergraduate classes, graduate classes and the Frederick Conference Center.

The school offers more than forty majors, minors, concentrations, interdisciplinary and special programs for undergraduates and five graduate degrees. Graduate level certificate programs are also available. Every undergraduate participates in the Veritas Program, which is a common, four-year curriculum integrated with every academic major and includes leadership development and cultural components.

In 1988 the Mount moved to Division I status within the NCAA. To complement the booming athletic department, the university razed an old farm and barns on the east side of Route 15 and opened the new Knott Athletic Recreation Convocation Center (ARCC).

The Mount enrolled 1,842 undergraduate and 508 graduate students during the 2012-2013 academic year. The Seminary has 172 seminarians.

Drawing on its deep Catholic traditions, the Mount is deeply involved with the Emmitsburg and Frederick communities. From reading programs in area schools, to Habitat for Humanity, campus food drives for local food banks, to visits to nursing homes, Mount students contribute more than 23,000 hours of direct service to local, regional, national and international organizations each year.

✧

Above: Located on the campus of Mount St. Mary's, the National Shrine Grotto of Our Lady of Lourdes is the oldest American replica of the famous French shrine. In 1965 the Pangborn Memorial Campanile was dedicated and Cardinal Shehan of Baltimore proclaimed the site a public oratory (inset). Today the shrine welcomes more than 400,000 visitors to Frederick County each year.

Below: Athletics are an integral part of student life at Mount St. Mary's. In 1962, students celebrated when the men's basketball team won the NCAA championship (inset). In 1988 the Mount moved to Division I, and currently has sixteen teams including men's and women's lacrosse, tennis, basketball, cross country, track and field (indoor and outdoor), baseball, softball, and women's soccer and swimming.

Plamondon Companies

A simple, four word mission statement sums up the Plamondon Companies approach to business. Those four words—'The Values You Respect'—are simple and concise, but instill the ideas that form the backbone of the company.

Founded in 1980, Plamondon Companies operates 50 Roy Rogers Restaurants in 9 states, including 21 corporate locations and 29 franchise locations. In addition, the company operates six Marriott brand hotels including Fairfield Inn & Suites, Courtyard, TownePlace Suites and Residence Inn in Frederick; as well as SpringHill Suites and Courtyard in Hagerstown. The company also manages the Hampton Inn & Suites Fort Detrick.

Plamondon Companies is truly a family business. Several generations of Plamondons have been involved in the hospitality business, starting with the parents of Pete Plamondon, Sr., who moved from Chicago to Vero Beach, Florida, in 1946 to buy a thirty-six room hotel/motel on the beach. Pete, Sr., worked at the motel as a kid and enjoyed it so much he decided to study hospitality in college.

Pete, Sr., became an executive with Marriott Corporation, and was instrumental in establishing the Roy Rogers brand and restaurant project. He decided to start his own business in 1980 when he opened a Roy Rogers Restaurant on U.S. 40 in Frederick.

Plamondon's sons, Pete, Jr., and James, were involved with the family business from the very start. Pete, Jr., who was twenty years old at the time, worked as an assistant manager in the first restaurant, and Jim, still in high school, handled janitorial chores. Pete, Sr., dreamed of becoming a successful franchisee and owning a handful of Roy Rogers Restaurants in the Frederick and Loudoun Counties area. At the time, neither of the sons intended to be involved in the restaurant business, but this would change.

Pete, Jr., graduated from Cornell University in 1981, worked in Marriott's hotel division for several years, and then spent eight years as a commercial real estate broker in Washington, D.C. After gaining valuable professional experience, he joined his dad's company in 1993.

Jim earned a BA degree from Notre Dame University in 1985, followed by a law degree from the George Washington University's National Law Center in 1988. He worked as an associate in a private law firm and as an Assistant U.S. Attorney for the District of Columbia before joining the family business in 1995.

Just prior to the time Pete, Jr., and Jim joined the family business, Marriott decided to sell the Roy Rogers brand to Hardees Restaurants in order to focus its efforts on hotels. At the time, there were about 648 Roy Rogers Restaurants in the nation, with 184 located in the Baltimore/Washington area. Hardees was primarily a Southern and Midwestern company and the meshing of the company culture with the Roy Rogers brand did not go smoothly.

Meanwhile, the Plamondon family was considering ways to grow beyond restaurants and decided to return to their roots in the hotel business with Marriott. They understood the Marriott culture and business model well and were approved to open a Fairfield Inn by Marriott in 1996. The hotel was the first new hotel to open in Frederick County in many years.

Pete, Jr., and Jim purchased Plamondon Enterprises from their parents in 1998 and became co-presidents of Plamondon Companies. Following the success of their first hotel, the company opened Courtyard by Marriott in 1999. That property performed very well, aided by the move of Bechtel into same office park, and in 2002, Residence Inn by Marriott was opened.

By this time, Hardees had given up on the Roy Rogers brand and was selling the restaurant real estate in the Washington region, largely to McDonalds. Realizing that the trademark and franchise system was up for grabs, the Plamondons decided it was time to fix the neglected, but well-loved restaurants, and bring the Roy Rogers brand back to life. At the time, only about eighty Roy Rogers Restaurants still existed. A decision was made to get rid of the poorly-performing locations and start selling new franchises. This decision was rewarded in December 2001, when the first franchise opened in Germantown, with lines of excited customers streaming out the door.

So many individuals have contributed to the success of Plamondon Companies over the years it would be impossible to list them all. However, two men should be singled out. On the restaurant side, Mike Boyd, who had been a district manager for Marriott's Roy Rogers division, helped develop Plamondon Enterprises' franchise efforts. On the hotel side, Michael Henningsen, who had been general manager of a Marriott in Rockville, became director of hotel operations for Plamondon.

Plamondon Companies now employs 860 people and is headquartered at 4991 New Design Road in Frederick. Pete, Jr.'s daughter graduated recently from the hotel school at Virginia Tech and his two sons are studying at Cornell's hotel school, raising the possibility that there may soon be a fourth generation active in the family business.

Pete, Sr., is still involved in the business and is a great cheerleader for his sons. He often shares his belief that if you hire the right people and trust them and their ideas, the best thing is to get out of their way.

Plamondon Companies has grown as Frederick County has grown over the last decade. The challenge for Pete and Jim is to keep the culture and mission statement alive as the business grows and extends beyond the Frederick County borders.

ImQuest BioSciences, Inc.

ImQuest BioSciences, Inc., founded in 2004, is a full-service contract research laboratory that provides preclinical research and development services to the biotechnology and pharmaceutical industry.

ImQuest specializes in the areas of infectious disease, cancer, inflammatory disease, and pharmaceutical product development. In the infectious disease area, ImQuest focuses on the development of drugs, biologics and vaccines for the treatment of HIV, hepatitis B and C, dengue virus, herpes viruses, influenza and other respiratory virus infections, and cancer, as well as development of prevention products for sexually transmitted diseases. ImQuest also develops products for the treatment of bacterial infections such as drug resistant bacteria and Clostridium difficile. The firm's cancer programs include capabilities to develop therapies for a wide variety of solid and hematopoietic tumors.

The core group that organized ImQuest had worked together at other companies in the Frederick and Germantown area. After nearly fifteen years in the contract research organization (CRO) business, Dr. Robert W. Buckheit, Jr., was looking for opportunities to create his own CRO, which would provide higher levels of professional and scientific services to companies he had worked with for most of his career.

Dr. Buckheit found the seed money necessary to begin the laboratory in Frederick and, within six months, the company was able to sign enough contracts to be financially stable and profitable. Daniel Caffoe, who now serves as chairman of the board of directors, was very instrumental in the founding of the company, along with the founding professional staff of Karen Watson Buckheit, M.S.; Tracy Hartman, M.S.; Todd Parsley, Ph.D; and Lu Yang, M.D.

In the firm's early days, the six person staff worked out of Dr. Buckheit's home. They also personally helped prepare the initial laboratory facilities by painting, putting down floor tile, upgrading lighting and moving lab furniture and equipment into a 4,500 square foot space at 7340 Executive Way in Frederick. ImQuest now occupies nearly 11,000 square feet in this location.

Several important contracts helped ImQuest grow from the very beginning. An exclusive licensing agreement with Samjin Pharmaceutical Co. Ltd. of Seoul, South Korea, included development of a series of compounds as inhibitors of HIV. Two of these compounds progressed to clinical trials as an HIV therapeutic and as a topical microbicide to prevent the sexual transmission of HIV. A second agreement with Samjin called for development of a series of molecules for various forms of cancer, and an exclusive agreement with Samjin granted ImQuest exclusive first rights to develop any new products for the treatment of infectious disease and cancer. The firm also signed an agreement with California-based ISIS Pharmaceutical, Inc., to develop a product for the treatment of HIV.

ImQuest's initial strong growth was stressed by the global economic collapse of 2007-08, but the firm responded to those challenging times by mixing work for biotechnology and pharmaceutical industry clients with millions of dollars in NIH grants to support the development of infectious disease products.

✧

Right: Dr. Robert Buckheit received the Medium Established Company Entrepreneur of the Year award from the Entrepreneur Council of Frederick County in 2011.

Below: Dr. Buckheit meets with distinguished scientists from Samjin Pharmaceutical Co. Ltd. of Seoul, South Korea, as they negotiate a partnership to co-develop new drugs for AIDS and other infectious diseases and cancer. The Samjin-ImQuest deal successfully launched ImQuest's drug development programs in 2005. Samjin and ImQuest have continued to work together on these important projects through 2013.

Among those individuals responsible for ImQuest's growth and development were Tracy Hartman, who led the infectious disease efforts, which were highly profitable during the firm's early days; Karen Watson Buckheit, who has led the topical microbicide and women's health programs since the firm's inception; and Dr. Anthony Ham, who was hired in 2010 for his ability to formulate drugs into novel delivery vehicles such as transdermal patches and vaginal gels.

A second generation of the Buckheit family began working with ImQuest during the period from 2005 to 2008, gaining valuable experience for their future careers. Dr. Buckheit's son, Robert W. Buckheit III, went on to earn a Ph.D. degree from Johns Hopkins University, while his daughter, Christa Buckheit Sturdevant, obtained her Ph.D. degree from the University of North Carolina at Chapel Hill. A third Buckheit sibling, Megan Buckheit, also worked for ImQuest before pursuing her passion for elementary school education, and she now teaches in Montgomery County, Maryland.

ImQuest has grown from five employees in 2004 to the current staff of twenty-two employees. Annual revenues total approximately $4.6 million from biotechnology, pharmaceutical and academic laboratories, as well as from research grants from the National Institutes of Health.

The firm has received a number of awards from local and state organizations and was named Small Business of the Year by the Tech Council of Maryland in 2010. Dr. Buckheit was named Entrepreneur of the Year in 2011 by the Entrepreneur Council of Frederick County and ImQuest was named one of Frederick's Best Places to Work in 2012 by the Frederick County Office of Economic Development.

ImQuest employees are involved in a number of community and charitable activities, including St. Jude's Children's Cancer Research Center and an internship program for high school students interested in the sciences. The firm is the primary host/sponsor of a local Frederick County biotechnology networking group, the 'BioBeers'. Annual team participation in the Polar Bear Plunge benefits the Maryland Special Olympics. Dr. Buckheit was the head coach of the JV soccer team at Middletown High School from 2000 to 2008. While in this role, he established an internship program for Middletown students with an interest in pursuing a career in the sciences.

Looking to the future, ImQuest hopes to develop several products which will successfully transition to human clinical trials and hopefully be approved as products to treat or prevent transmission of infectious viruses, bacteria, and/or cancer. They also hope to maintain their business in Frederick to the point that a younger generation of scientists may take over the company and lead it forward for another generation.

Above: The ImQuest scientific team enjoys a relaxing and fun-filled day celebrating the company being named one of Frederick County's Best Places to Work in 2012. "We work very hard at ImQuest, but we always take the time to celebrate our successes and reward our employees for a job well done!" said Dr. Buckheit. Top row, left to right: Bob Buckheit, Amanda Helfrick, Tracy Hartman, Christian Furlan-Freguia, Sean Nugent, Anthony Ham and Caitlin Buchholz. Bottom row, left to right: Gail Larkins, Karen Buckheit, Maggie Garvey, and Lu Yang.

Left: ImQuest scientists Karen Watson Buckheit and Ashlee Boczar work in the laboratory with infectious AIDS virus as they develop an important ImQuest microbicide product to prevent the sexual transmission of the virus. ImQuest's microbicide product is scheduled to begin clinical trials in 2014.

Millennium Financial Group, Inc.

In only ten years, Millennium Financial Group, Inc.—better known as Mlend—has built a strong reputation as an outstanding mortgage lender offering "Home Loans Made Fast & Easy" to customers throughout the Mid-Atlantic region.

Mlend was organized in October of 2003 by William Hunt Poffenbarger, Jr., who was born and raised in Woodsboro, Maryland, and attended Walkersville High School. After graduating from the University of Oklahoma, Poffenbarger was working for Southwestern Bell, now AT&T, and had relocated his family from Dallas, Texas, back to his roots in Frederick County, building a home for his family in Middletown, Maryland, where he currently resides.

A friend of Poffenbarger's in Oklahoma presented an opportunity in mortgage lending that he decided to pursue. The opportunity resulted in a Maryland location as a mortgage broker. After working as a broker for six short months, Poffenbarger decided to open Millennium Financial Group, Inc., and pursue the ability to lend money for mortgages, not broker those funds. The controls and quality stamps that can only be achieved with the lender designation were essential to Poffenbarger's business plan.

The firm officially transitioned from broker to lender in 2005, just two short years after incorporating and received licenses to operate in Maryland, Pennsylvania, West Virginia, Virginia, Delaware, North Carolina, Florida, and the District of Columbia.

"Taking care of the client should be the number one objective of every business," says Poffenbarger. "At Mlend, we have built our business around this simple fundamental. We don't stand under the apple tree waiting to eat; we nurture the tree, fertilize it, and harvest the apples consistently. Our customers need the same treatment, well thought-out lending solutions that exceed their expectations while maintaining competitive pricing. We put customers in the best product for their short-term and long-term needs by listening, asking the right questions, and thoroughly examining their unique situation."

As a full-service lender, Mlend employs dedicated mortgage consultants and an experienced in-house support team to offer expertise in every area of mortgage financing: Buy A Home, Refinance, or Use Home Equity.

Mlend provides a full range of mortgage products and the firm's mortgage consultants are dedicated to placing their customers in the "Right" loan—with the best rates, terms and costs—to meet each client's unique borrowing needs. Mlend experts communicate with their clients through each step of the loan process by providing regular updates and progress reports.

Mlend currently offers the following Mortgage Loan Programs: Federal Housing Administration, Veterans Affairs (VA), U.S. Department of Agriculture, and Conventional.

Mlend underwrites, closes, and funds more than ninety-eight percent of the loans they offer to their clients. The company has also earned "FHA Direct Endorsement Lender" status, given only to lenders in the industry who meet strict guidelines. These guidelines include review of the company's experience, sound lending practices, financial strength, and overall business conduct.

Today, Mlend is still headquartered in Middletown, Maryland, and operates retail branch offices in Crofton, Frederick, and Middletown, Maryland; Fairfield and York, Pennsylvania; and Morgantown, West Virginia. The company is currently licensed to transact lending business within five states in the Mid-Atlantic region: Maryland, Virginia, West Virginia, Pennsylvania, Delaware and the District of Columbia.

The company founder, Poffenbarger, remains the owner and president, Brandy Mosser is vice president and treasurer, Karen Goodyear is secretary and Teresa Keener is the Director of Underwriting.

The company has grown from only a few employees a decade ago to around forty-five today. Mlend and its employees are deeply involved in local community activities, including the United Way, Middletown Valley Athletic, Middletown High School Boosters, Mid-Maryland Basketball, and Mountain Valley Youth Football League.

We realize that home financing is one of the largest financial decisions anyone makes in their lifetime. Whether you are a first time homebuyer, refinancing your existing home, or moving to your dream home, our mortgage consultants and support team are committed to making your home financing experience "Fast & Easy!"

In Loving Memory of Fordham Lee Poffenbarger (2005-2010).

Fordham Lee is adored by his parents, sister and brothers, and continues to live in heaven with God and in the hearts of his extended family and close friends who cherish his short time here on this earth. We love you Fordham Lee.

National Fallen Firefighters Foundation

✧

To Lift a Nation created by sculptor Stan Watts, to honor the heroes of September 11, 2001.

To firefighters around the nation and the world, Frederick County, and specifically Emmitsburg, is an extremely well known place. It is where they come to enhance their fire service education from renowned instructors at the National Fire Academy. It is where the fire service and our nation honor the firefighters who have given their lives in the line of duty. It is also the home of the National Fallen Firefighters Memorial.

The Memorial was created in 1981. In 1990 it was recognized by Congress as the official monument to all fallen firefighters. Two years later Congress created the National Fallen Firefighters Foundation (the Foundation) to lead a nationwide effort to remember these American heroes.

The Foundation's offices are located in the National Fallen Firefighters Memorial Chapel on the grounds of the National Fire Academy in Emmitsburg. The campus was originally a boarding school for girls founded by St. Elizabeth Ann Seton. It later became St. Joseph's College, one of the first Catholic colleges for women in the United States. In 1973 the Daughters of Charity closed the college and sold the buildings and land to the federal government.

Each October thousands of firefighters and members of the public gather in Emmitsburg for the National Fallen Firefighters Memorial Weekend. Hundreds of firefighters and volunteers help the families and friends of those who died in the line of duty the previous year. The Candlelight Service on Saturday evening and the Memorial Service on Sunday morning help the survivors celebrate the lives of their loved ones. The Foundation provides reassurance that these survivors and their firefighters will not be forgotten.

During the Memorial Service, the names of those who are being honored are added to the National Fallen Firefighters Memorial. The memorial features a Maltese Cross, the traditional symbol of the fire service, and an eternal flame at the base. It is surrounded by brass plaques that include the names of the honored firefighters. The Memorial Service is open to the public so that anyone can pay tribute to the fallen and their loved ones. Thousands of people, including members of Congress, Administration officials and other dignitaries, families, friends, and coworkers of the fallen firefighters attend annually.

In addition to the Memorial Weekend, the Foundation sponsors conferences and workshops for adult survivors and camps for the children of the fallen. A scholarship program is also available through the Foundation to help the spouses, life partners, children and stepchildren of fallen firefighters pursue their educational goals.

The Foundation is committed to reducing the number of line-of-duty deaths that occur annually. The Everyone Goes Home® program was created to address the need for change within the fire service, promoting safe practices, so that Everyone Goes Home®. The Foundation hosts meetings and training programs on the National Fire Academy campus throughout the year and provides educational programs and assistance to fire departments nationwide.

In addition to the National Fallen Firefighters Memorial, visitors to the campus can also see the forty foot tall bronze monument, *To Lift a Nation*, that was created by sculptor Stan Watts to honor the heroes of September 11, 2001. The three-times life-size statue recreates the now-famous photo taken by Thomas E. Franklin, a photographer for the *Bergen Record*, who captured the image of three firefighters raising the American flag at Ground Zero.

The Memorial Park features a brick Walk of Honor® that connects the monument, the historic Fallen Firefighters Memorial Chapel, and memorial plazas. Each brick on the walkway bears a personal inscription. In 2011 a brick plaza and ten sections of walkway were installed in front of the sculpture. The addition of this new branch of the Walk of Honor® completes part one of a three part park development project to expand the Walk of Honor® to connect the National Fallen Firefighters Memorial and the historic Memorial Chapel to the 9/11 sculpture. We invite you to visit the Memorial. It is open year round from dawn to dusk.

The National Fallen Firefighters Foundation takes great pride in the commitment and dedication of our neighbors in Emmitsburg and Frederick County who help us honor the men and women whose names are part of this important national monument.

✧

Above: The historic National Fallen Firefighters Memorial Chapel.

Below: The National Fallen Firefighters Memorial.

The City of Frederick

The City of Frederick, Maryland's second largest city provides residents with a balanced and thriving economy, a highly educated workforce and an enviable quality of life. Located less than an hour from Washington, D.C., and Baltimore; The City of Frederick is the county seat of Frederick County and the hub of arts, culture, commerce and government within the county.

Frederick Town was laid out in 1745 by land speculator Daniel Dulany, who attracted German immigrants from eastern Pennsylvania to settle his planned village on Maryland's western frontier. These people were joined by English and Scots-Irish people who came from southern Maryland. Frederick Town quickly became a burgeoning crossroads of commerce and craftsmanship. In addition, Frederick Town's importance would grow as it became the seat of county government in 1748.

The City of Frederick had become an important market town by the latter part of the eighteenth century, as well as one of the leading mining areas in the nation. Gold, copper, limestone, marble, iron and other minerals were mined nearby and, by the start of the American Revolution, The City of Frederick was a leading iron producer. New transportation routes passed through the region, extending opportunities for natural resources, agricultural products, and manmade goods to reach larger markets. The early nineteenth century saw the construction of the National Road, Baltimore & Ohio Railroad and Chesapeake & Ohio Canal. With these innovations, The City of Frederick would also see many new faces in town as visitors benefitted from better roads and railways.

Because The City of Frederick was a major crossroads, both Union and Confederate troops marched through the town during the Civil War, headed toward such decisive battles as Antietam and Gettysburg. The Battle of Monocacy, the 'battle that saved Washington' was fought just south of town only hours after Frederick paid a Confederate ransom of $200,000. After the battles, The City of Frederick became a major hospital center. Today it is home to the National Museum of Civil War Medicine.

The City of Frederick continued to grow as a center of agriculture and commerce during the twentieth century and soon became one of Maryland's largest cities. Today, The City of Frederick is the second largest city in the state, with a population of 65,000. That represents a growth rate of nearly twenty-four percent between 2000 and 2010.

The City of Frederick's proximity to Washington has always been an important factor in the local economy and has greatly affected the City's growth in recent years. Because of the location of Fort Detrick, the City's main employer, The City of Frederick has become a center for cancer research and is also strongly influenced by several other industries, including bioscience, technology, education, government, healthcare, banking, tourism and others.

The City of Frederick's award-winning fifty-block historic district, neighborhoods and diverse industry base offer residents and visitors a unique blend of history and technology. The City of Frederick celebrates the arts and has been named by *American Style Magazine* as a "Top 25 Small Arts City" in the United States. The City of Frederick's Historic Downtown and neighboring fifty-four acre Baker Park play host to special events on twenty-two weekends each year, including summer concerts, gallery walks and theatrical performances.

Frederick County Bank

Frederick County Bank (FCB), an independent full-service community bank with a commitment to serving the Frederick County market area, was formed in 2001 by a group of local business leaders including John N. Burdette, now chairman emeritus of the board, and Raymond Raedy, the principal organizer and current chairman of the board. In announcing plans for the new financial institution, Burdette explained, "Frederick County Bank has been formed for the purpose of serving the County's business and professional community which has been underserved by the out-of-area banks that are coming into the Frederick County market. FCB will provide the personalized banking services which many local customers need and demand."

FCB reached its minimum regulatory capital amount of $7 million in just fifty-two days and opened its first two bank centers in October 2001, followed by two additional locations in September 2007. FCB's newest bank center opened in January 2012 and is located on the East side of Frederick City near the airport. FCB has experienced steady growth since operations commenced and has posted positive quarterly earnings continuously since 2002. The bank's holding company, Frederick County Bancorp, Inc., became effective in September 2003. FCB reported net income of $1.4 million for 2012 and assets of $320 million at the end of the first quarter of 2013.

As a true community bank, Frederick County Bank is proud to provide clients the superior customer service, individual attention and timely decision-making they deserve. The bank currently employs more than seventy people who have more than 1,000 years of combined experience in the banking industry. FCB offers a comprehensive suite of personal and business banking products and services designed to assist clients in achieving their unique financial goals, including checking and savings accounts; online and mobile banking with bill pay; consumer loans, mortgages and home equity lines of credit; cash management solutions for businesses; and other valuable products for increased online security and fraud protection. In addition, FCB is the only bank in Maryland that offers a business courier service to collect non-cash business deposits for same-day processing, saving local business owners time and money.

With a defined vision of building relationships that empower employees, exceed clients' expectations, and enrich the communities served by FCB, the bank formed a community action committee in 2010 to identify volunteer opportunities with local nonprofit organizations and encourage employees to participate in service-related activities. In 2012, eighty-two percent of FCB's employees participated in more than 450 community service activities to support a wide variety of worthy causes, including the Downtown Frederick Partnership, the Community Action Agency's Soup Kitchen, Habitat for Humanity, the Community Foundation of Frederick County, the American Cancer Society, Big Brothers Big Sisters, and many more. In addition, FCB hosts three free community shred days at its bank centers each year in order to help Frederick County residents protect themselves against identity theft and fraud.

For more information, visit www.fcbmd.com.

WELOCALIZE

✧

Below: Smith Yewell, CEO Welocalize.

PHOTOGRAPH COURTESY OF REBECCA FAY.

BOTTOM: PHOTOGRAPH COURTESY OF ANDREW MURDOCK, NATURAL ARTISTRY.

Welocalize, one of the country's most unique and fastest growing companies, translates websites and marketing materials into more than a hundred languages on demand to give global companies local relevance.

The company was started sixteen years ago by the husband and wife team of Smith and Julia Yewell in the basement of their home. According to company CEO Smith Yewell, it all started with one word. "Our first job from a paying customer was to translate the word 'pathfinder' into a half-dozen languages," he explains. That one word initiated a chain reaction that changed the way translation services were delivered forever. Welocalize has now translated more than a billion words and continues to discover new ways of getting translation projects done.

Welocalize provides translation services that help company's market software originally produced for English-speaking customers in foreign markets.

"A lot of people misunderstand what we do," comments Yewell. "We don't make translation software. We're translating their software. Take Microsoft Word. If Microsoft needs it in German, we translate it into German and engineer any needed changes, and then return the product to Microsoft, which can then market it to the German-speaking market."

Following a business plan that declares, "We do things differently," Welocalize posted 181 percent fiscal year growth during the period from 2006 to 2011. The company's core values include the 'Four Pillars' of customer satisfaction, quality, innovation and teamwork.

Welocalize operates with an operational excellence strategy that commits employees to building a company that relies on creativity, innovation and teamwork to drive productivity in everything it does.

Welocalize, with more than 600 employees worldwide, has been headquartered in Frederick's Glass Factory building since 1999. The company maintains offices in Boston, Massachusetts; Portland, Oregon; San Mateo, California; Seattle, Washington; Dublin, Ireland; Cheshire, United Kingdom; Beijing, China; Jinan, China; and Tokyo, Japan.

Welocalize's customer base includes such major firms as Google, Microsoft, Dell, John Deere and NetApp. The company recently received *Inc. Magazine*'s Top 500 Companies designation for the eighth year in a row.

Yewell feels the success of Welocalize can be attributed to a company culture that values each individual employee. "We are about people," he says. "Our culture is very important to us and we believe in work/life balance. We believe in everyone voicing their opinion so we can work together and make things better."

Welocalize's executive team consists of Founder and CEO Smith Yewell, Chief Operations Officer Eugene McGinty, Chief Administrator Officer Tim Delbrugge, Senior Vice President-Supply Chain and Production Business Units Olga Blasco, Senior Vice President-Global Sales Erin Wynn, and Vice President-Technology and Professional Services Derek Coffey.

FREDERICK MUTUAL INSURANCE CO.

The rich heritage of Frederick Mutual Insurance Co. is intertwined with the history of Frederick County and the growth of the property and casualty insurance business in America.

Founded by an act of the Maryland legislature in 1843, Frederick Mutual Insurance Company was established to protect Frederick County residents from fire loss to their homes, farms and businesses. Originally named the Mutual Insurance Company of Frederick County, the firm issued its first policy on May 1, 1844, and paid its first fire loss in 1845.

One of the company's early policyholders was Barbara Fritchie, one of the central figures in Frederick County's history. At the age of ninety-five, so the story goes, Fritchie stood in the road and waved the Union flag as Confederate General Stonewall Jackson led his troops through Frederick during the Civil War.

The incident inspired poet John Greenleaf Whittier to write: "'Shoot if you will this old gray head; but spare your country's flag,' she said."

The original office location at 44 North Market Street served the company until it moved to 114 North Market Street in 1924. The company's name was changed to Frederick Mutual Insurance Company in 1993 and land was purchased for a new Home Office at 57 North Thomas Johnson Drive in 1994. An addition—the Nicodemus Wing—was added in 2006.

Over more than 170 years, Frederick Mutual has evolved into a financially sound property and liability carrier represented by agents throughout Maryland and Pennsylvania. The company offers insurance of various types through a network of professional independent insurance agents. Products offered by the company include Homeowners, Dwelling Fire, Personal Umbrella, Business Owners, Artisan Contractors and Commercial Umbrella.

The company currently has policyholders in both Maryland and Pennsylvania, providing property and casualty coverage for homeowners, renters and small businesses. Plans call for Frederick Mutual to expand to three additional states by 2020.

Frederick Mutual is a strong supporter of giving back to the community and its employees are involved in such organizations as the Community Foundation of Frederick County, Salvation Army, Frederick Rescue Mission, Frederick County ARC, Frederick County Mental Health Association, Frederick Memorial Hospital, Hood College, Frederick Community College, Mount Saint Mary's University and many others.

Frederick Mutual is a strong, reliable insurance company with more than $50 million in assets. The company is rated A- (excellent) by A. M. Best, the most widely recognized insurance company rating organization. In the past fifteen years, the company has grown from $5 million in written premiums to $24 million.

Hampton Inn Frederick

You will find everything you need for a relaxing, comfortable stay at the Hampton Inn Frederick, located off Interstate 270 at 5311 Buckeystown Pike.

You will feel right at home in a comfy guest room with cable TV, microwave, lap desk, hairdryer, iron with board, refrigerator and free high-speed Internet. You can start your day right with Hampton's free hot breakfast, including our famous waffles and a wide array of hot and cold items.

A spacious work desk and seating area are provided in all rooms at the Hampton Inn Frederick. Each room is warmly decorated and includes a coffee maker and clock radio. All guests have free access to the outdoor pool and twenty-four hour fitness center.

A business center is located on site with fax, printer, and photocopying service. You may reserve meeting space in one of our flexible meeting rooms with accommodations for up to fifty participants. If you are planning a larger reception, you can reserve the ballroom with space for up to 200 attendees.

Whether you prefer Mexican, French, Chinese, Thai or Good Old American cuisine, you will find restaurants galore within a short distance of the Hampton Inn. Applebees, Bob Evans, Cracker Barrel, Dutch's Daughter, Golden Corral, Griff's, Jerry's Subs, Romano's Macaroni Grille and aka Frisco's are just a few of the many area restaurants.

The Hampton Inn Frederick is surrounded by a town that boasts a rich and fascinating history. The National Museum of Civil War Medicine is less than three miles away. You will not have to look far to see the famous spires immortalized in the poem *Barbara Fritchie*. The Weinberger Center for the Arts has a wide variety of offerings, from drama to music. The Francis Scott Key Monument is located in Frederick and the author of our national anthem is buried in the town. Three separate museums are dedicated to the C&O Canal, the B&O Railroad, and the history of horse-drawn carriages in the United States. We also recommend you visit the grounds of the Armed Forces Retirement Home, where President Abraham Lincoln drafted the Emancipation Proclamation.

When you have explored all the historical things to see near our hotel, catch a performance at one of the local nightclubs, enjoy an AA baseball game or go hiking or biking on one of the town's many trails.

The Hampton Inn Frederick received the 2013 *TripAdvisor* Certificate of Excellence Award, an honor awarded to establishments that achieve outstanding traveler reviews on *TripAdvisor*, the world's largest travel site. This award recognizes the great pride in which our staff consistently offers an exceptional experience to our guests.

For more information about the Hampton Inn Frederick, please check their website at www.frederick.hamptoninn.com.

Historical Society of Frederick County

Founded in 1892, the Historical Society of Frederick County is one of the oldest and most honored heritage preservation organizations in Maryland. The Historical Society is a 501(c)(3) nonprofit educational organization made up of individuals, families, and businesses—people like you—who come together for the common purpose of preserving our community's history and sharing that history with people of all ages and backgrounds.

Over its long history, the Historical Society has evolved from a small group meeting in the homes of its members to the truly countywide organization it is today. During this time the Historical Society's collections of books, documents, and artifacts have grown to become the most complete and comprehensive assemblage of Frederick County materials in existence.

The Historical Society had a number of homes until 1959 when it purchased the Federal-style building on Church Street in Frederick that it now occupies. Built by Dr. John Baltzell in 1820, the home subsequently was residence to the Hanson and Loats families. In 1882 the home became an orphanage and more than 100 Frederick County girls called the building home until the facility closed in 1956.

Today, the Historical Society operates two museums and a research facility all regularly open to the public. The Museum of Frederick County History features local history through guided tours and changing exhibitions. The Roger Brooke Taney House tells the story of the county's early nineteenth century inhabitants, free and enslaved, and the life and career of Roger B. Taney, fifth U. S. Chief Justice. The Frederick County Archives and Research Center possesses the finest collection of historical and genealogical materials available to research county histories and families. The Historical Society also offers a diverse schedule of educational programs for children and adults, engaging activities, school programs, downtown walking tours, and special events throughout the year.

The Historical Society has attained several important achievements and honors in recent years, including the accreditation of its museum by the American Alliance of Museums. In 2006 the Historical Society was presented with the award for Outstanding Commitment to the Preservation and Care of Collections, a national award putting it in the company of others such as Colonial Williamsburg and the National Archives and Records Administration.

The Historical Society of Frederick County draws on its deep ties to the community by offering high quality programs and services that impact the lives of county residents and visitors. The Historical Society invites all to "Discover History Here!" Begin your discovery of Frederick County's history on the Historical Society's website at www.frederickhistory.org. Here you will find information on hours of operation, directions to various locations and special events.

Rebecca Pearl Gallery

✧

Clockwise, starting from the top:

Rebecca loves her gallery and her German Shepherds.

Wilderness Fox.

Glimpse of Yesteryear.

Snow White Grill.

Rebecca Pearl is a well known artist in and around Maryland. Originally from Philadelphia, she is the daughter of James Pearl who was a self made Jewish graphic designer for over fifty years. She began drawing in her father's studio at age four and has never stopped. The artist studied fine art at the Maryland Institute College of Art and The Schuler School in Baltimore.

At age twenty-two Pearl became a licenced practical nurse and worked full or part time for twenty-eight years. This enabled her to do her art on days off or at night and continue to grow in skill and experience. In 1990 Pearl opened an art gallery in a now trendy part of Baltimore called Hampden. This provided her a place to showcase her work meet with customers and take commissions from the public. Over the years the Pearl has concentrated on painting her surroundings, historic architecture, street scenes, old barns and places on the battlefields. Because of her love of animals she has developed a market of old world portraits of dogs, cats and horses.

After living in Baltimore for twenty-three years she moved back to Frederick County where she had gone to high school and still had many family members. Renting a small house in New Market, she began painting the quaint old places that quickly caught on in the community. Since then the artist has created a large collection of images reflecting the history of Frederick County. They are captured in watercolor, pastel, or oil in a semi-impressionistic style that is easily recognized as a "Rebecca Pearl".

Currently the artist resides on a small farm near Emmitsburg, Maryland. She has painted many landmarks close by including scenes of Mount St. Mary's University campus, the Grotto of Lourdes, and portraits of Saint Elizabeth Ann Seton. In 2004 Pearl delivered a painting of Seton to Pope John Paul II in Rome just before he died. Pearl has completed a series of historic paintings surrounding Thurmont, the home of the Cozy Restaurant, and the Camp David Museum. She is married to James Zeigler, her high school sweetheart, who is also a partner in the Rebecca Pearl Gallery and master framer.

Pearl teaches painting in her gallery to people of all ages and experience and enjoys sharing acquired knowledge and skill with others. In the past six years the artist has illustrated seven childrens books in collaboration with authors Lois Noffsinger and Dawn Hull including her own book, *Gilbert and the Great Horse Spirit*. At sixty-five Pearl enjoys her country life with her husband, 3 German shepherds, and 3 horses. She often says, "All this and Heaven too?", a quote from Elizabeth Ann Seton, who started the first parochial school in America in 1808.

The Rebecca Pearl Gallery is located in Emmitsburg. Please visit www.rebeccapearl.com or call 301-788-1875 for more information. Email: rebeccapearl123@gmail.com.